READINGS ON

JANE EYRE

THE GREENHAVEN PRESS
Literary Companion
TO BRITISH LITERATURE

READINGS ON

JANE EYRE

Jill Karson, *Book Editor*

David L. Bender, *Publisher*
Bruno Leone, *Executive Editor*
Bonnie Szumski, *Series Editor*

Greenhaven Press, Inc., San Diego, CA

Every effort has been made to trace the owners of copyrighted material. The articles in this volume may have been edited for content, length, and/or reading level. The titles have been changed to enhance the editorial purpose. Those interested in locating the original source will find the complete citation on the first page of each article.

Library of Congress Cataloging-in-Publication Data

Readings on Jane Eyre / Jill Karson, book editor.
     p.   cm. — (The Greenhaven Press literary companion to British literature)
    Includes bibliographical references and index.
    ISBN 0-7377-0176-5 (pbk. : alk. paper). —
ISBN 0-7377-0177-3 (lib. : alk. paper)
    1. Brontë, Charlotte, 1816–1855. Jane Eyre.
I. Karson, Jill. II. Series.
PR4167.J5K377   2000
823'.8—dc21

Cover photo: Stock Montage, Inc.

Copyright © 2000 by Greenhaven Press, Inc.
PO Box 289009
San Diego, CA 92198-9009
Printed in the U.S.A.

"I *care for myself. The more solitary, the more friendless, the more unsustained I am, the more I will respect myself.*"

—*Charlotte Brontë*, Jane Eyre

Contents

Chapter 1: Structure and Symbolism in *Jane Eyre*

Natural setting represents psychological conditions in *Jane Eyre*, a novel in which the organization is more akin to poetry than conventional fiction.

Fire and water imagery support the heroine's main conflict: that Jane must temper the "fire" of lust without succumbing to the icy "waters" that would destroy all passion.

The five homes featured in *Jane Eyre* serve as a structural and thematic device: Gateshead, Lowood, Thornfield, Moor House, and Ferndean all mark clear stages in Jane's education and moral development.

The three pictures painted by Jane symbolically represent major stages in Jane's development. The first picture represents Lowood, while the second and third pictures prophesy her experiences at Thornfield and Marsh End.

Chapter 2: *Jane Eyre*'s Narrative

The heroine tells her own story in *Jane Eyre*. Although many critics find this narrative method inadequate, Brontë presents her story with such skill that she overcomes the disadvantages traditionally attributed to first-person narration.

FOREWORD

*"'Tis the good reader that
makes the good book."*

Ralph Waldo Emerson

The story's bare facts are simple: The captain, an old and scarred seafarer, walks with a peg leg made of whale ivory. He relentlessly drives his crew to hunt the world's oceans for the great white whale that crippled him. After a long search, the ship encounters the whale and a fierce battle ensues. Finally the captain drives his harpoon into the whale, but the harpoon line catches the captain about the neck and drags him to his death.

A simple story, a straightforward plot—yet, since the 1851 publication of Herman Melville's *Moby-Dick*, readers and critics have found many meanings in the struggle between Captain Ahab and the whale. To some, the novel is a cautionary tale that depicts how Ahab's obsession with revenge leads to his insanity and death. Others believe that the whale represents the unknowable secrets of the universe and that Ahab is a tragic hero who dares to challenge fate by attempting to discover this knowledge. Perhaps Melville intended Ahab as a criticism of Americans' tendency to become involved in well-intentioned but irrational causes. Or did Melville model Ahab after himself, letting his fictional character express his anger at what he perceived as a cruel and distant god?

Although literary critics disagree over the meaning of *Moby-Dick*, readers do not need to choose one particular interpretation in order to gain an understanding of Melville's

9

novel. Instead, by examining various analyses, they can gain numerous insights into the issues that lie under the surface of the basic plot. Studying the writings of literary critics can also aid readers in making their own assessments of *Moby-Dick* and other literary works and in developing analytical thinking skills.

The Greenhaven Literary Companion Series was created with these goals in mind. Designed for young adults, this unique anthology series provides an engaging and comprehensive introduction to literary analysis and criticism. The essays included in the Literary Companion Series are chosen for their accessibility to a young adult audience and are expertly edited in consideration of both the reading and comprehension levels of this audience. In addition, each essay is introduced by a concise summation that presents the contributing writer's main themes and insights. Every anthology in the Literary Companion Series contains a varied selection of critical essays that cover a wide time span and express diverse views. Wherever possible, primary sources are represented through excerpts from authors' notebooks, letters, and journals and through contemporary criticism.

Each title in the Literary Companion Series pays careful consideration to the historical context of the particular author or literary work. In-depth biographies and detailed chronologies reveal important aspects of authors' lives and emphasize the historical events and social milieu that influenced their writings. To facilitate further research, every anthology includes primary and secondary source bibliographies of articles and/or books selected for their suitability for young adults. These engaging features make the Greenhaven Literary Companion series ideal for introducing students to literary analysis in the classroom or as a library resource for young adults researching the world's great authors and literature.

Exceptional in its focus on young adults, the Greenhaven Literary Companion Series strives to present literary criticism in a compelling and accessible format. Every title in the series is intended to spark readers' interest in leading American and world authors, to help them broaden their understanding of literature, and to encourage them to formulate their own analyses of the literary works that they read. It is the editors' hope that young adult readers will find these anthologies to be true companions in their study of literature.

INTRODUCTION

Jane Eyre follows the orphan Jane, who, despite restricting circumstances, triumphs over adversity through the strength of her character. On one hand, Jane is plain and diminutive—a shadow of obscurity. Yet Brontë's forceful narrative and soaring imagination transmute the orphan into a strong and fiery woman, fiercely determined as she struggles, through a range of emotional experience, to find happiness while preserving her moral integrity.

Brontë's narrative is powerful for a number of reasons. For one, many of Jane's travails were drawn directly from events and feelings that Brontë herself experienced—her own tormented love affair, for example, or her painful religious crises. The result is a powerful and passionate web of autobiographical material and fiction. Too, Brontë found in prose—unlike in her poetry, which is usually considered mediocre—the perfect vehicle to give full sway to her romantic and poetic spirit. *Jane Eyre*, then, is much more than an ordinary novel; it is a work of artistry, a gripping drama infused with moral significance and rich poetic beauty.

Critic E.F. Benson once called *Jane Eyre* a "tissue of violences, absurdities, and coincidences," and indeed many critics have described the plot as improbable and highly sensational: Rochester's concealment of a dangerous, lunatic wife under Jane's very roof, for instance, seems artificial and contrived, and Jane's falling on the very doorstep of her unknown relatives almost strains readers' credibility. Yet these apparent weaknesses do not encumber the novel. Even the most hostile critics—and *Jane Eyre* has provoked many—cannot deny the fire of Brontë's genius. Just as it mesmerized Victorian readers, *Jane Eyre* continues to enthrall and challenge modern readers who find the combination of Jane's passionate nature and ferocious ethic irresistible.

The Greenhaven Press Literary Companion to British Literature: Jane Eyre presents a wealth of information to aid the

reader of this provocative work. The volume opens with a biography of Charlotte Brontë that includes a discussion of
how she challenged Victorian standards, making her one of
the most distinctive writers of her day. A wide range of critical essays, written in the context of Brontë's era and modern
times, lend insight into *Jane Eyre*'s many layers of meaning
and recurring themes. Other selections highlight elements of
plot, structure, and narrative. Finally, a plot synopsis,
chronology, and bibliography make this an accessible and
comprehensive tool for readers wishing to know more about
Brontë's *Jane Eyre*, one of the greatest novels of the nineteenth century.

CHARLOTTE BRONTË: A BIOGRAPHY

Charlotte Brontë was born April 21, 1816, the third child of Maria Branwell Brontë and the Reverend Patrick Brontë, a minister of the Church of England. Her siblings included Maria, born in 1814; Elizabeth, born in 1815; Patrick "Branwell," born in 1817; Emily, born in 1818; and Anne, born in 1820. Charlotte spent most of her life in her father's parsonage in Haworth, Yorkshire, in northern England. Typical of small nineteenth-century industrial towns, Haworth was cramped and dirty; few dwellings had outhouses and sewage polluted the streets. Disease flourished. Yet the sweeping moorlands stretched just beyond the Brontës' parsonage. This dramatic natural landscape provided the Brontë children with not only a vast playground but also a welcome reprieve from the town's squalor. Years later, in *Jane Eyre*, Charlotte's destitute heroine would find tranquility in the peaceful, unadulterated moorlands.

EARLY LIFE

When Charlotte was five, her mother died of stomach cancer. For the next several years, the Reverend Brontë, aided by his strict and pious sister-in-law Elizabeth Branwell, cared for the children. The young Maria also played a prominent role in nurturing the other Brontë children, who found in their eldest sister a kind and gentle mother figure.

In 1824, Patrick sent Maria, Elizabeth, Charlotte, and Emily to the Cowan Bridge School, a boarding school for the daughters of clergymen. Charlotte endured extremely harsh conditions at Cowan Bridge, including poor sanitation, freezing temperatures, and inadequate food. Moreover, several mean-spirited teachers mistreated the students. In 1825, Maria and Elizabeth contracted tuberculosis, a contagious and often fatal disease that flourished in crowded and dirty conditions. After their deaths, Patrick sought to spare his other daughters the same fate and withdrew Charlotte and Emily from the school. Yet her experiences at Cowan Bridge left a bitter, lifelong impression on Charlotte, who characteristically wove autobiographical material into her fiction. As a novelist, she would vent her deep anger, using Cowan Bridge as a basis for *Jane Eyre*'s terrible Lowood School.

YOUTHFUL WRITINGS

Charlotte remained at Haworth until 1831. During these years, her father and aunt guided the children's education and exposed them to a wide variety of reading material. At the same time, Patrick and Aunt Branwell, as the children called her, left the children ample opportunity for creative pursuits. With their fertile imaginations, Charlotte and her precocious siblings had no trouble entertaining themselves. The children read avidly—Charlotte had read most of Byron's complete works by the age of twelve—and also loved to romp across the windy moors. When, in 1826, Patrick presented Branwell with a box of toy wooden soldiers, the children eagerly incorporated these "Young Men" into their imaginative play. Each child claimed a soldier—Charlotte called hers the Duke of Wellington—and began spinning fantastic tales, replete with monsters, dungeons, and great adventures. The children recorded these stories in various forms, noteably as handprinted tiny manuscripts, too small for an adult's eye. The children were quite prolific; in the first year they compiled eighteen tiny books.

More than a hundred of these tiny volumes survive. The subject of scholarly study, these youthful writings provide a glimpse of the collective Brontë literary genius. As Brontë biographer William Stanley Braithwaite notes:

> The Brontë children, before and even during adolescence, made this writing into a game in which the materials were wholly of the mind and the emotions. The language in which they recorded and communicated the experiences of their "Young Men" is shot through with the same beauty and flame that ultimately was to crystallize into the superb romances of Charlotte's Angria and the Angrians. . . . No better practice fields could be devised for the writing of such classics as *Jane Eyre*.[1]

Growing out of her adventures with her "Young Men," Charlotte, in cahoots with Branwell, conceived a mythical kingdom located on the coast of Africa, which they called Angria. The young writer gave her imagination free rein as she recorded the adventures of the Duke of Zamora and other colorful characters. The Angrian sagas enabled Charlotte to immerse herself in her writing and transcend the limitations of her own life—the family lived in near poverty and Charlotte never fully recovered from her sisters' deaths, among other hardships. At the same time, the Angrian tales further refined her maturing storytelling abilities. Before Charlotte could make her mark in the literary community, however, the young writer needed to go back to school.

ROE HEAD

In 1831, Patrick sent Charlotte to Roe Head School in Mirfield, some twenty miles from Haworth. After her grim experience at Cowan Bridge, Charlotte found Roe Head pleasant and comfortable. At first, however, Charlotte's simple clothing and her rather unbecoming physical appearance—she was small and plain, much like the heroine of *Jane Eyre*—made her feel inferior to some of the other pupils. Even without robust good looks and a graceful demeanor, however, the willful Charlotte soon proved to students and faculty that she possessed a keen intellect and sterling character. She not only earned several prizes for scholarship, but also formed two particularly close friendships with pupils Mary Taylor and Ellen Nussey, the latter of whom preserved over four hundred of Charlotte's letters, a rich source of information for future Brontë biographers.

At sixteen years of age Charlotte returned to Haworth in 1832. For the next several years, Charlotte oversaw the education of Branwell, Emily, and Anne. She spent her time on long walks in the nearby moors and also continued to read and write, producing a series of romantic if not fantastic tales in the vein of Byron, her childhood hero. Perhaps Charlotte's passion for fantasy freed her from a rather dreary existence, for as Charlotte described these times in a letter to Ellen Nussey: "In the morning, from nine o'clock till half-past twelve, I instruct my Sisters and draw; then we walk till dinner, after dinner I sew till tea time, and after tea I either read, write, do a little fancy work or draw, as I please. Thus, in one delightful, though somewhat monotonous course, my life is passed."[2]

CHARLOTTE THE TEACHER

In July 1835, hoping to ease the family's financial burdens, Charlotte accepted a teaching position at the Roe Head School. She soon found, however, that she did not relish the experience; her teaching duties were overly restrictive and the huge workload tortuous. Yet for nearly three years, Charlotte persevered, feeling duty-bound to remain at the school. As time passed, she became increasingly distraught and guilt-ridden. In a letter to Ellen Nussey, Charlotte described her feelings:

> I *do* wish to be better than I am. I pray fervently sometimes to be made so. I have stings of conscience—visitings of remorse—glimpses of Holy, inexpressible things, which formerly I used to be a stranger to. . . . Do not mistake me, Ellen, do not think I am good, I only wish to be so, I only hate my former flippancy and forwardness. O! I am no better than I ever was. I am in that state of horrid, gloomy uncertainty.[5]

Charlotte finally left the school in 1838.

In addition to her guilt at having failed as a teacher, other events during this period caused Charlotte distress. For one, she feared that her sister Anne, whose health was never robust, might succumb to the same disease that claimed the lives of her sisters Maria and Elizabeth. Charlotte also worried about Branwell's increasingly errant behavior. Jobless and naturally high-strung, Branwell indulged in what was considered—especially in Victorian times—reckless and immoral pursuits: loitering in taverns, womanizing, and drinking heavily.

Moreover, Charlotte was deeply disappointed when she sent several poems to Robert Southey, poet laureate of England. In Southey's negative assessment, Charlotte's verses were overly imaginative. He warned the young writer that "literature cannot be the business of a woman's life, and it ought not to be. The more she is engaged in proper duties, the less leisure will she have for it, even as an accomplishment and a recreation."[4]

Despite Southey's discouraging words, Charlotte maintained faith in her writing ability and steadfastly eschewed the "proper duties" befitting a Victorian woman, including marriage. During this period, a resolute Charlotte rejected two proposals from local clergymen. She did, however, make an attempt at being a governess. Finding the work boring, menial, and beneath her, she eagerly relinquished one governess position after another. It is not surprising that years later, Charlotte's character Jane Eyre, a plain and lowly governess, would embody her own frustrations over the dismal career options available to unmarried Victorian women.

Unfulfilled as a teacher or governess and distressed by the family's pressing financial troubles, Charlotte conceived a plan to open a school in Haworth. When her aunt offered to finance the endeavor, Charlotte convinced her that first, she and Emily must journey abroad to finish their education. In February

1842, the two sisters headed to the Pensionnat Heger in Brussels, an experience that would change Charlotte's life.

BRUSSELS

To Charlotte and Emily, who had never ventured far from home, Brussels offered exciting new cultural experiences. Perhaps more importantly, Charlotte came in contact with Monsieur Constantin Heger, the demanding but highly intelligent headmaster of the school. Heger recognized the sisters' extraordinary talents and arranged private lessons during which he would read aloud masterpieces of French authors. Among other pieces of advice, he told the two young women, "It is necessary, before sitting down to write on a subject, to have thoughts and feelings about it. I cannot tell on what subject your heart and mind have been excited. I must leave that to you."[5]

These words must have had a profound impact on Charlotte, who deeply admired Heger's fiery intellectual passion. Charlotte, in fact, was falling in love with Heger. Although no one knows for certain what transpired between the two, the love affair was one-sided—Heger was married and did not return Charlotte's intense, amorous feelings. Nonetheless, her encounter with Heger radically influenced Charlotte's later fiction. Many of her experiences with Heger would be described in both *The Professor* and *Villette*. Certainly, too, Charlotte's great romantic character Edward Rochester bears a striking resemblance to the swarthy, black-haired Heger, whom Charlotte called "a little black ugly being . . . a man of power as to mind, but very choleric and irritable in temperament."[6]

In November 1842, learning that their aunt had died, Emily and Charlotte returned to Haworth. While Emily chose to remain at home, Charlotte returned to Brussels the following January. Charlotte's obsession with Heger was growing; at the same time she realized that her love was unrequited. Lonely and distraught, a heartbroken Charlotte left Brussels for good in the fall of 1843. Back at the parsonage, Charlotte wrote Heger poignant love letters, only to receive platonic replies in return. As usual, Charlotte took refuge in her writing, expressing her anguish in poetry:

> He saw my heart's woe, discerned my soul's anguish,
> How in fever, in thirst, in atrophy it pined;
> Knew he could heal, yet looked and let it languish,
> To its moans spirit-deaf, to its pangs spirit-blind.[7]

To add to Charlotte's misery, Branwell was growing more

wayward. Having failed to establish a career for himself, he spent most of his time and money on alcohol and opium. Also disappointing was the sisters' failed attempt, in 1844, to establish the school they had envisioned several years earlier. Not one student responded to their initial advertisement.

Charlotte's spirits lifted somewhat in the fall of 1845, when she discovered some poetry written by Emily. She considered it excellent and conceived a plan to publish a book of verse that would include her own poetry as well as Emily's and Anne's. The sisters chose to use ambiguous pseudonyms to mask their gender and thereby avoid the Victorian prejudice against women writers. As Charlotte explained years later in her "Biographical Notice" in the second editions of Emily's *Wuthering Heights* and Anne's *The Tenant of Wildfell Hall:*

> Averse to personal publicity, we veiled our own names under those of Currer, Ellis, and Acton Bell; the ambiguous choice being dictated by a sort of conscientious scruple at assuming Christian names positively masculine, while we did not like to declare ourselves women, because—without at that time suspecting that our mode of writing and thinking was not what is called "feminine"—we had a vague impression that authoresses are liable to be looked on with prejudice; we had noticed how critics sometimes use for their chastisement the weapon of personality, and for their reward, a flattery which is not true praise.[8]

In 1846, Charlotte, Anne, and Emily published, at their own expense, *Poems* of Currer, Ellis, and Acton Bell. The use of pseudonyms did not guarantee the success of the work, however; the Brontë's first book sold only two copies. It did, however, generate some favorable reviews. One unnamed reviewer wrote: "It is long since we have enjoyed a volume of such genuine poetry as this. Amid the heaps of trash and trumpery in the shape of verses . . . this small book . . . has come like a ray of sunshine, gladdening the eye with present glory and the heart with promise of bright hours in store."[9]

Heartened by such enthusiastic reviews, the Brontës were undaunted by lack of sales. As Charlotte later wrote about the project: "The mere effort to succeed had given a wonderful zest to existence, it must be pursued."[10]

THE CREATIVE YEARS

The three sisters soon embarked on their first novels: Emily on *Wuthering Heights,* Anne on *Agnes Grey,* and Charlotte on *The Professor,* a story that chronicles her experiences in Brussels and speculates on what might have been had she won Heger's love. Both *Wuthering Heights* and *Agnes Grey* were quickly accepted by publishers, but *The Professor* received only rejections. (It would be published posthumously in 1857.) Nonetheless, Charlotte was cheered when the manuscript reached a Mr. Williams of the firm of Smith and Elder. Although Williams, too, rejected *The Professor*, his cordial reply expressed a desire to view the author's future work. Encouraged by Williams's response, Charlotte, who had already started *Jane Eyre*, finished the novel that would catapult her to fame.

On August 24, 1847, Charlotte sent Smith and Elder her completed manuscript. One of the owners of the firm, George Smith, took the manuscript home and—as thoroughly captivated as many readers would be—read the entire novel in one sitting. *Jane Eyre* was immediately accepted for publication.

JANE EYRE

Jane Eyre, presented as the autobiography of Jane Eyre written by Currer Bell, electrified the literary community. The novel's first review appeared in the *Atlas:* "This is not merely a work of great promise, it is one of absolute performance. It is one of the most powerful domestic romances which has been published for many years. . . . It is a book to make the pulses gallop and the heart beat, and to fill the eyes with tears."[11] Demand for the novel was so resounding—Victorian readers devoured the book as popular entertainment—that it was reprinted only three months after its initial publication. Charlotte—or Currer Bell, as she called herself—was famous.

The beauty and power of Charlotte's writing certainly account for much of *Jane Eyre*'s popularity. Yet the novel was extraordinary for other reasons. In writing *Jane Eyre*, Charlotte challenged the conventions of her generation, particularly the Victorian emphasis on propriety. In Jane, Charlotte created a straightforward and sensual female character. Her passionate romance with the lusty Rochester shocked many critics, who found the novel indecent, coarse, and somewhat immoral. As Brontë biographer Charlotte Maurat explains: "In Victorian society at that time, vice was as a matter of fact carefully concealed beneath a mask of hypocrisy. And so this story, whose passion and realism suddenly broke with the accepted tradition, was considered disconcertingly bold and shockingly crude by a section of the public, who nevertheless went on reading it!"[12]

REVEALING THE BELLS' IDENTITY

Victorian readers' enthrallment with *Jane Eyre* sparked increasing curiosity about the novel's author. The speculation intensified when Ellis Bell's *Wuthering Heights* and Acton Bell's *Agnes Grey* finally came out in print. Thus far, the sisters, in addition to using pen names, had kept their writing ventures secret even from family and close friends. Rumors that the Bells were brothers of a weaving fraternity in Lancashire or that the three Bells were actually one person swept through the literary community.

Meanwhile, Charlotte began writing *Shirley*, while Emily and Anne started their second novels. In June 1848, Anne's *Tenant of Wildfell Hall* was published, again under the pseudonym Acton Bell, fueling more confusion as to the Bells' identity. To rectify the situation, Charlotte and Anne traveled to London to meet their publishers in person and thereby prove their separate identities.

Despite *Jane Eyre's* spectacular success, family tragedy soon marred Charlotte's happiness. Branwell was dying of tuberculosis. Anne and Emily, too, appeared unwell. Shortly after Branwell died in September 1848, the family recognized in Emily the familiar symptoms of the deadly disease that had claimed Branwell's life—severe congestion and a hacking cough. Day by day, Charlotte watched helplessly as her sister wasted away. Emily died in December 1848. Soon after, in May of 1849, Anne, too, succumbed to the disease.

Charlotte was utterly crushed by the deaths of her siblings. Perhaps her writing sustained her through this bleak period; even in her distraught state, she completed *Shirley*, an attack on society's treatment of women and workers. *Shirley* was published in October 1849 and, although the reviews were less laudatory than those of *Jane Eyre*, the book sold well.

Over the next several years, Charlotte traveled frequently to London, enjoying the friendship of the famous, including critic George Henry Lewes, feminist social critic Harriet Martineau, novelist William Makepeace Thackeray, and Elizabeth Gaskell, who would become Charlotte's official biographer. She also began a fourth novel, titled *Villette*. In 1850, both to honor her sisters and to clear up any lingering confusion regarding authorship, she composed a memorial preface to the second editions of her sisters' novels.

THE FINAL YEARS

A series of illnesses took their toll on Charlotte during the final four years of her life. Among other health problems, she suffered a severe liver infection as she finished *Villette*, which, set at a girls' school in Villette, features the memorable heroine Lucy Snowe. *Villette* was published to favorable reviews in 1853.

In 1854, she married the Reverend Arthur Bell Nicholls, her father's curate at Haworth. The newlyweds made their home in the parsonage and, for a brief time, Charlotte reveled in domestic tranquility. Nicholls was a devoted husband who lavished attention on his bride. Despite her newfound happiness, however, Charlotte's health remained frail. Once, she became dangerously ill after being drenched in a sudden rainstorm. Her physical condition worsened when she became pregnant in early 1855. By early spring, it was clear that Charlotte had contracted tuberculosis. Weeks of fever, coughing, and painful nausea wasted her slight frame. Charlotte and her unborn child died on March 31, 1855. She was thirty-nine years old.

NOTES

1. William Stanley Braithwaite, *The Bewitched Parsonage: The Story of the Brontës.* New York: Coward-McCann, 1950, p. 37.
2. Quoted in T.J. Wise and J.A. Symington, *The Shakespeare Head Brontë: Life and Letters,* vol. 1. Oxford: The Shakespeare Head Press, 1931, p. 103.
3. Quoted in Wise and Symington, *The Shakespeare Head Brontë,* vol. 1, p. 103.
4. Quoted in Bettina L. Knapp, *The Brontës: Branwell, Anne, Emily, Charlotte.* New York: Continuum, 1991, p. 37.
5. Quoted in Lyndall Gordon, *Charlotte Brontë: A Passionate Life.* New York: W.W. Norton, 1994, p. 98.
6. Quoted in Gordon, *Charlotte Brontë,* p. 94.
7. Quoted in Rebecca Fraser, *The Brontës: Charlotte Brontë and Her Family.* New York: Crown, 1988, p. 243.
8. Charlotte Brontë, "Biographical Notice of Ellis and Acton Bell," *Wuthering Heights.* New York: Random House, 1943, p. vi.
9. Quoted in Miriam Allott, *The Brontës: The Critical Heritage.* London: Routledge & Kegan Paul, 1974, p. 59.
10. Quoted in Fraser, *The Brontës,* p. 260.
11. Quoted in Allott, *The Brontës,* p. 67.
12. Charlotte Maurat, *The Brontës' Secret.* New York: Barnes & Noble, 1970, p. 179.

CHARACTERS AND PLOT

LIST OF CHARACTERS

Mr. Brocklehurst. The mean-spirited and hypocritical founder of Lowood School who publicly declares that Jane is a liar.

Helen Burns. The devout and scholarly student who befriends Jane Eyre at Lowood School.

Jane Eyre. The heroine of the novel. The daughter of a poor clergyman, Jane is orphaned and left in the care of her unloving and overly critical aunt, Mrs. Reed.

Alice Fairfax. The kind and motherly housekeeper at Thornfield.

Blanche Ingram. The beautiful but shallow young woman who tries to lure Edward Rochester into marriage.

Bessie Lee. Jane's childhood nurse employed by Mrs. Reed; her small gestures of affection help sustain Jane throughout her miserable tenure at Gateshead Hall.

Bertha Mason. Edward Rochester's mad wife, kept locked away in a third-story room at Thornfield Hall; her occasional night wanderings mystify Jane, who, until her wedding day, is unaware of Bertha's existence.

Dick Mason. Bertha's brother, who interrupts the wedding of Jane and Edward Rochester.

Rosamund Oliver. The shallow and flirtatious young woman who finances the girls' school at Morton.

Grace Poole. The eccentric servant who feeds and cares for Bertha Mason at Thornfield Hall.

Eliza Reed. Mrs. Reed's oldest daughter; she becomes a nun after Mrs. Reed's death.

Georgiana Reed. Mrs. Reed's beautiful but spoiled and vain younger daughter.

John Reed. Mrs. Reed's cruel son, who torments Jane at every opportunity; he grows up to be a ne'er-do-well.

Mrs. Sarah Reed. The cold, critical, and mean-spirited aunt who makes Jane's early life unbearable.

Marie and Jane Rivers. The benevolent sisters of St. John Rivers who welcome Jane into their family.

St. John Rivers. The zealous vicar of Morton who, although he is in love with Rosamund Oliver, tries to persuade Jane to become his wife and assist him with missionary work in India.

Edward Rochester. The son of a wealthy landowner who is tricked into marrying the insane Bertha Mason; he falls in love with Jane despite his circumstances.

Maria Temple. The kind and generous headmistress and superintendent of Lowood School.

Adele Varens. The daughter of a French opera dancer who was once Rochester's mistress; she is Jane's charge at Thornfield.

Plot Summary

The penniless orphan Jane Eyre lives with her aunt and uncle, the Reeds, and her three cousins, John, Eliza, and Georgiana. When Mr. Reed dies, Mrs. Reed treats Jane like an unwelcome guest, abusing and neglecting her niece while unabashedly spoiling her own children. On their part, John, Eliza, and Georgiana never miss an opportunity to berate and torment the desolate Jane. When she rebels against this mistreatment, Jane is locked in the red room where her uncle had died nine years before. Here, Jane imagines that she sees her uncle's ghost. Jane's tortured screams summon the family and servants, who listen to her cries for pity through the locked door. When her pleas to be freed go unheeded, Jane faints and later awakens in her own bed, where the servant Bessie tenderly nurses her. Because of the extreme fright she has endured, Mr. Lloyd, the apothecary, is called to examine Jane. He suggests that Jane would be happier at a boarding school.

The forbidding Mr. Brocklehurst, headmaster of the Lowood School for Girls, comes to Gateshead to interview Jane. When Jane refuses to be intimidated by the narrow-minded and pious Brocklehurst, Mrs. Reed leads the headmaster to believe that Jane is deceitful and in need of harsh discipline. In retaliation, Jane threatens to expose her aunt's ill deeds to the residents of Lowood.

Jane, forlorn, leaves for Lowood School. Only Bessie bids her farewell. Upon arrival, Jane observes the dismal conditions in which students are forced to live: The food is meager and often inedible, the work schedule is grueling, and the surroundings are cheerless. Moreover, the shoddy buildings provide little protection against the unrelenting winter cold. Despite the many physical deprivations, Jane settles into the spartan routine and delights in the friendship offered by a kindly student, the virtuous Helen Burns. Jane is also uplifted through her association with a supportive and generous teacher, Miss Temple. Another teacher, Miss Scatcherd, however, is particularly abusive. Jane is distressed when Miss Scatcherd treats the undeserving Helen with special cruelty. Yet Helen is stoic and bears her trials with fortitude. Further, Helen comforts the devastated Jane after Mr. Brocklehurst announces to the school that Jane is a liar. Miss Temple, too, sustains Jane by announcing to the school that Jane has been falsely accused.

With the arrival of spring, conditions slightly improve at Lowood. Students are permitted to romp outdoors in the outlying woods. Jane even makes a new friend, Mary Ann Wilson. This brief peaceful interlude is short-lived, however, when a typhus epidemic strikes the school. Jane learns that Helen Burns is dying and, despite the threat of contagion, visits Helen in her last moments. The epidemic draws public attention to the poor conditions at Lowood, which fosters many reforms at the school. Jane spends eight more years at Lowood, the last two as a teacher. When Miss Temple marries and moves away, Jane becomes restless and accepts a governess position at Thornfield Hall. Just before she departs, Jane meets Bessie, a servant from Gateshead, who reveals that the Reed family is not prospering and also that seven years earlier, a Mr. John Eyre, Jane's uncle, called at the Reeds on his way to Madeira.

Jane arrives at Thornfield Hall close to midnight. The mansion appears warm and inviting despite its great size. Jane is greeted by the congenial Mrs. Fairfax, who she learns is the housekeeper of Edward Rochester, whose eight-year-old ward, Adele Varens, is to be Jane's student. As Jane tours her new home, she hears a mirthless laugh emanating from the third floor. She is told that it is Grace Poole, a reclusive servant who lives in the attic. Later, when she is out walking, Jane offers to help a rider who has fallen from his horse. On her return, she is summoned by her employer, whom she recognizes as the fallen rider.

Jane is immediately attracted to her brusque and moody employer. In turn, Rochester is impressed by Jane's quiet honesty and intellect. As time goes on, the two become friends. One day, Rochester explains that Adele is the illegitimate daughter of his former mistress, French opera dancer Celine. Although he does not acknowledge Adele as his biological child, he has adopted her out of kindness. That night, Jane hears the sinister laugh again and discovers that Rochester's room is on fire. She bravely extinguishes the flames with water. Rochester encourages Jane to believe that the fire was caused by Grace Poole.

Jane hides her disappointment when, the next day, Rochester leaves the house. Several weeks later he returns with a party of guests, including the beautiful but snobbish Blanche Ingram, with whom Rochester openly flirts. Even though she finds Blanche shallow and inferior to Rochester, Jane surmises the two will marry. As a result, Jane—although she is now deeply in love with Rochester—forces herself to give up her romantic daydreams.

While Rochester is away on business, a mysterious stranger named Mason arrives. Soon after, Rochester returns, disguised as a gypsy fortune-teller. He speaks to each of his houseguests, and also to Jane, who is very careful in her responses to the gypsy's probing questions. Later that night, Jane hears bloodcurdling shrieks. She discovers that Mr. Mason has been stabbed, it seems by Grace Poole. Jane alone helps Rochester tend to the man's wounds.

Soon after, Bessie's husband, John Leaven, arrives to inform Jane that John Reed is dead and that Mrs. Reed has suffered a stroke and wishes to see her. When she visits Gateshead, she finds her cousins as self-centered and discourteous as ever. Jane learns, too, that three years prior, her Uncle John from Madeira had sent a letter stating his intentions of making Jane his heir. The still bitter Mrs. Reed confesses that she lied to John Eyre, telling him that Jane had died at Lowood.

After Mrs. Reed's death, Jane returns to Thornfield. Although she predicts Rochester's impending marriage to Blanche, she confesses to him that she is overjoyed to be home. On a midsummer's eve, Rochester declares his love for Jane and the two agree to marry. Only a violent thunderstorm and Mrs. Fairfax's anxious looks foreshadow trouble ahead.

Jane—despite her impending marriage—remains a governess until her wedding day. She also writes to her uncle, hoping that someday she will have some money of her own. On the eve of the wedding, however, Jane grows apprehensive. She is troubled by frightening dreams and awakens to find a dark and savage-looking woman tearing her wedding veil in two. The next day, during the wedding ceremony, two strangers interrupt the service to deliver some startling news: The wedding cannot proceed because Rochester is already married. Thus, Jane learns that the mysterious figure at Thornfield is Bertha Mason, whom Rochester married fifteen years earlier. Rochester explains how he was tricked into marrying the hideously insane woman and how he keeps her in a secret apartment on the third floor of Thornfield, under the care of Grace Poole. Jane is shattered. Despite Rochester's desperate pleas that he still loves her and that she should become his mistress, Jane, mired in grief, slips away from Thornfield in the early dawn.

After two days of travel, Jane, now destitute, wanders hungry and exhausted through the countryside. After dark, she stumbles on a house known as both Moor House and Marsh End. Its occupants, St. John Rivers and his gentle sisters, Mary and Diana, take in Jane, now known as Jane Elliott, and nurse her back to health. St. John is handsome and possesses admirable qualities, but Jane finds him somewhat cold and self-serving. Jane, Mary, and Diana, though, discover mutual interests and enjoy one another's company. At month's end, however, the two sisters must leave to work as governesses. St. John installs Jane as a schoolmistress in a school financed by the flirtatious heiress Rosamund Oliver, with whom St. John shares a mutual attraction. Jane encourages St. John to marry Rosamund but he declines, finding her frivolous nature unsuitable to the missionary work he hopes to pursue abroad.

Eventually, St. John discovers Jane's true identity and learns about events at Thornfield. Not only are Jane and the Rivers cousins, but Jane's uncle, John Eyre of Madeira, has died and left her an inheritance. Jane generously shares the sum with her three cousins.

St. John admires Jane's fortitude and strong work ethic. As he prepares to travel abroad, he urges Jane to join him as his wife and assistant. Jane knows that it would not be a marriage born of love, however, and declines. Persisting with his moral arguments, St. John almost convinces Jane to acquiesce. Suddenly, however, she hears Rochester's phantomlike voice calling her name. The next day, she sets out for Thornfield.

Jane is devastated to see Thornfield in ruins, burnt to the ground. She learns that her old home was destroyed by a fire started by Bertha Mason, who plunged to her death during the blaze. In his efforts to save her, Rochester lost his eyesight and the use of one hand. Jane finds him at his isolated country home in Ferndean. There, Rochester and Jane declare their love and the two are married immediately.

Ten years later Jane concludes her story: She lives in perfect happiness with Rochester, who partly recovers his sight in time to see his firstborn child. Adele matures into a fine woman, Diana and Mary Rivers happily marry, and Jane is comforted by the thought that St. John, near death in India, will enjoy a heavenly reward.

CHAPTER 1

Structure and Symbolism in *Jane Eyre*

READINGS ON
JANE EYRE

Jane Eyre: Dramatic Poetry

Mark Schorer

In his introduction to the Houghton Mifflin edition of
Jane Eyre, Mark Schorer identifies several flaws in the
novel, including a highly implausible plot and a structure that he calls "nearly artless." Schorer argues,
nevertheless, that the novel should not be judged according to traditional views of structure. Rather, the
rich poetic imagery that pervades the story—especially the natural landscapes—renders *Jane Eyre* a
form of dramatic poetry as opposed to conventional
realistic fiction. As a poetic novel, then, *Jane Eyre* is a
compelling and finely crafted work of art.

[*Jane Eyre*] was accepted enthusiastically by the first publisher to read it, and it appeared on August 24, 1847, as *"Jane
Eyre: An Autobiography*, edited by Currer Bell." It was an instant triumph and has remained one, especially with female
readers, ever since. Why?

THE NOVEL'S FLAWS

Its weaknesses are obvious and have long been observed.
The action is pitted with implausibilities, indeed, absurdities. The account of the manners of an aristocratic life with
which the author was unfamiliar is childish. The notion that
a man can for years conceal a raging maniac in the attic of
his house and keep even the servants ignorant of her presence there, especially since he is so unwise as to put her under the care of a gin-tippling attendant whose stupors permit
her frequently to escape the attic and range cursing through
the house, is truly ridiculous. To dress up one's hero in the
skirts and shawls of an old gipsy fortune teller and let him
woo the heroine in that guise in his own house is to risk at
least the loss of his Byronic austerity. To turn one's orphaned

Excerpted from Introduction, by Mark Schorer, © 1959 by Mark Schorer, to *Jane Eyre*,
by Charlotte Brontë (Boston: Houghton Mifflin, 1959).

heroine out into the world alone, subject her to the most frightful physical and emotional ordeals, and then let her stumble up to a house one night only to discover that its inhabitants are cousins of whose existence she had not known, and then to let her inherit a fortune besides—this is to challenge the reader to throw the book aside as unworthy of serious attention. But the reader does not throw the book aside, not even when the whole plot turns on an act of mental telepathy that brings the protagonists to their bitter-sweet embrace at last. Nor does he do so through all the crudities of the characterization, which is sometimes as gross as that in the baldest melodrama: the unadulterated malignity of Mrs. Reed, the unadulterated goodness of Helen Burns, the unadulterated malice of Miss Ingram—these are only examples. He reads to the end, for somehow the whole of the novel is compelling and strong even though so much of it is composed of these silly, feeble parts.

Is it, one might ask, the total artistry of the structure, the whole organization so firm that it welds even the limpest materials together, holds even coincidence and miracle firmly in place? Hardly. The structure of *Jane Eyre* is nearly artless. It employs, to begin with, one of the oldest conventions in English fiction, a convention made famous by Defoe's *Moll Flanders* (in which Charlotte Brontë may have found her source for the telepathic episode)—the fiction that presents itself as fact, the memoir of a presumably real person. Charlotte Brontë called this not a novel but an autobiography; the "real" author was Jane Eyre herself, and Currer Bell was merely her editor. Like *Moll Flanders*, *Jane Eyre* is, within this convention, very loosely put together; in both, events are linked not causally but circumstantially. Things happen to happen, they do not *have* to happen. Both novels begin at the beginning, cover a good stretch of time through a series of rather disparate adventures, and arrive at last at their happy endings. When we put them side by side in this way, we can see that there are similarities beyond those of structure; different as the rogue, Moll Flanders, may be from the pure governess, Jane Eyre, they are yet alike in a basic fact: each is a woman alone, making her way in a hostile world and making that world submit to her ways.

The comparison can be pressed no further, for *Jane Eyre* does have certain organizing principles that give it the dramatic coherence of a novel, and one cannot say this of *Moll*

Flanders. The action falls into four large blocks: the first ten chapters, which have to do with Jane's childhood and education, are introductory; the next seventeen chapters are concerned with her residence at Thornfield Hall, her developing love for its master, the collapse of their plans; the next

TRUTH AND NATURE

Few readers remain unmoved by Jane Eyre's *rich description of setting and natural phenomena. In his book* The Brontës and Nature, *Enid L. Duthie discusses Brontë's artistic commitment to the use of nature in her novels.*

It goes without saying that one of the major themes in *Jane Eyre* is nature, already so important in the juvenilia, and, though muted, still the source of what was most original in *The Professor.* But Charlotte Brontë confirmed its vital significance in her own formulation of her artistic credo, made in a letter to her publishers: "The first duty of an author is, I conceive, a faithful allegiance to Truth and Nature; his second, such a conscientious study of Art as shall enable him to interpret eloquently and effectively the oracles delivered by these two great deities." The "conscientious study of Art" was in fact almost completed when she returned from Brussels with an increased comprehension of the importance of form. *The Professor* was the last stage in her apprenticeship, and *Jane Eyre* the inspired performance of an artist sufficiently master of her form to be liberated from too close preoccupation with it. But her allegiance to "Truth and Nature" was a lifelong commitment and, in her view, they were complementary. She shared the belief of the Romantics that the poet possessed the power to discern the spiritual through the material, and to combine both in a new imaginative creation whose essential characteristic was, as G.H. Lewes had said of *Jane Eyre* on its first appearance, "reality—deep, significant reality".

It follows that the use of nature in *Jane Eyre* is intimately connected with the significance of the novel as a whole. From this point of view, as critics have increasingly recognized, the change of setting which accompanies each new stage in the action is essential to the portrayal of the heroine's development. . . . In *Jane Eyre* the five different settings represent no random selection but a planned and meaningful progression.

Enid L. Duthie, *The Brontës and Nature,* 1986.

eight chapters treat her flight, her life at Moor House and
Morton, and the icy proposals of St. John Rivers; the final
three chapters, returning her to Thornfield and a chastened
Rochester, resolve the whole. The second and third sections
are the heart of the book, and each of these is dominated by
a male who symbolizes one of the two polar forces between
which Jane's conflict is conducted. Rochester, licentious, re-
morseful, and handsomely ugly, is imperious physical passion; Rivers, chaste, self-righteous, and beautifully handsome, is equally imperious spiritual passion. Jane, who is
independent will, refuses to accept either on his own terms:
she will not be Rochester's mistress and she will not be
Rivers's wife; Rochester cannot marry her and Rivers will
not take her to India unless she marries him. The conflict is
resolved when Jane returns to Thornfield and finds that it
has been destroyed by a fire that killed Rochester's mad
wife, who had been the legal barrier to marriage, and
maimed Rochester himself in such a way as to suggest that
it has subdued his rampant sexuality and thereby removed
any ethical barrier. The conflicts here clearly represent Angrian extremities, and Richard Chase has quite neatly re-
ferred to them as "myth domesticated." One could say, too,
that *Jane Eyre* is fantasy rationalized.

Yet, important as it may be to know that the imagination
that created Angria [a fantasy kingdom created by Brontë as
a child] is likewise the imagination that created *Jane Eyre*,
and interesting as it may be to see how nearly the situations
and human types that struck the reverie of an adolescent girl
are those that are still most prominent in the mind of the
mature woman, one must yet recognize that we have tran-
scended Angria. What in the early writings we must call fantasy we can here call vision. A number of things have happened to bring about the change.

COMPLEX CHARACTERS

Most important of these, perhaps, is the difference in characterization. If some of the minor characters are one-dimensional,
the major characters are not. They are multi-faceted and of
a certain complexity. Rochester is not only the Byronic *im-
moraliste;* he is also a land owner, a man with certain economic and social responsibilities, with humor to lighten his
Ich-schmerz, and tenderness to soften his pride. St. John
Rivers is likewise a complex conception: at once kindly and

rigid, turbulent within and frigid without, in love and unyielding, he suffers from that spiritual pride that is the mark of the religious fanatic and that can lead as readily to martyrdom as to acts of inflexible cruelty. It is Jane Eyre herself, however, who represents Charlotte Brontë's triumph of characterization and who, in fact, brings a new kind of heroine into English fiction. If we think of her in relation to some of Jane Austen's heroines, for example, they may seem more engaging and desirable, but it is Jane Eyre who is motivated by desire itself. It is not only sexual desire—although that, remarkably enough, is obviously working through her conflicts—but a moral desire as well, and a moral desire of a new kind that is based on the frank recognition of a woman's need to find self-fulfillment in the world, in relations with others, especially men. This need gives the novel a nearly polemical bias:

> It is vain to say that human beings ought to be satisfied with tranquility; they must have action; and they will make it if they cannot find it. Millions are condemned to a stiller doom than mine, and millions are in silent revolt against their lot. Nobody knows how many rebellions besides political rebellions ferment in the masses of life which people earth. Women are supposed to be very calm generally: but women feel just as men feel; they need exercise for their faculties and a field for their efforts as much as their brothers do; they suffer from too rigid a restraint, too absolute a stagnation, precisely as men would suffer; and it is narrow-minded in their more privileged fellow-creatures to say that they ought to confine themselves to making puddings and knitting stockings, to playing on the piano and embroidering bags. It is thoughtless to condemn them, or laugh at them, if they seek to do more or learn more than custom has pronounced necessary for their sex.

Jane Eyre holds this view with *passion*, and passion is the key to her character. It is above all a passionate sense of the right of her own integrity to *be*. It breaks out first when, as a little girl, she tells Mrs. Reed that she does not like her; it breaks out most remarkably when, just before Rochester's proposal of marriage, she insists on her equality with him. It is the passion of Jane Eyre that imbues the whole novel—since it is all told from her point of view—and that animates those elements that give the whole its visionary quality. Similarly, it is the complexity that passion arouses in all these characters that gives the central ethical conflict a certain depth that enables us to take it seriously as we cannot take seriously the conflicts in Angria.

Another and hardly less important change lies in the fact that Angrian conflicts have been moved from imaginary lands of cloud into a real world, a world of social classes and institutions, no less than of natural landscapes. The presentation of manners may be naïve, but the observations on the injustices of charity schools, the hypocrisy of much religion, the cruelty of outmoded divorce laws, the vicious snobbery of a class system are all sound, and they enter into what we have already called the polemical bias of the book. So while the novel is chiefly concerned with subjective conflicts of a sometimes nearly hysterical order, these are substantially located in a social texture that is objective and mundane.

NATURAL SETTING

If society as here presented is in general at odds with the heroine's subjective ambitions for self-realization, the natural settings are, rather, reflective of their immediate state; as in most dramatic poetry, natural phenomena are the external representatives of psychological conditions. Natural setting, then, provides a kind of tenuous symbolic substructure to the novel, not only heightening but expressing thematic conflict. This technique, perhaps quite unconscious, is particularly observable in Charlotte Brontë's use of vegetation, especially the priapean tree—dormant, blasted, blossoming.

In that long wintry season that was Jane Eyre's youth, trees are bare; the second sentence makes the announcement: "We had been wandering . . . in the leafless shrubbery an hour in the morning." In her reveries, little Jane decides that no magic is left in England, that the elves "were all gone out of England to some savage country where the woods were wilder and thicker." The morning is a long one. Gateshead is perpetual winter:

> . . . the shrubbery was quite still: the black frost reigned, unbroken by sun or breeze, through the grounds. I covered my head and arms with the skirt of my frock, and went out to walk in a part of the plantation which was quite sequestered: but I found no pleasure in the silent trees, the falling fir-cones, the congealed relics of autumn, russet leaves, swept by past winds in heaps, and now stiffened together.

Lowood School is little better:

> . . . these beds were assigned as gardens for the pupils to cultivate, and each bed had an owner. When full of flowers they would doubtless look pretty; but now, at the latter end of Jan-

uary, all was wintry blight and brown decay. I shuddered as
I stood and looked round me ...

As for the forest on the banks of the Lowood stream, "*that*
showed only ranks of skeletons*.*" With Spring, as the time
approaches for Jane's departure for Thornfield, life blos-
soms with promise:

> and now vegetation matured with vigour; Lowood shook
> loose its tresses; it became all green, all flowery; its great elm,
> ash, and oak skeletons were restored to majestic life; wood-
> land plants sprang up profusely in its recesses; unnumbered
> varieties of moss filled its hollows . . .

It is as if the terms are being set for the presentation of
Rochester:

> "I have been green, too, Miss Eyre,—ay, grass green: not a
> more vernal tint freshens you now than once freshened me.
> My Spring is gone, however: but it has left me that French
> floweret on my hands; which, in some moods, I would fain be
> rid of. Not valuing now the root whence it sprang; having
> found that it was of a sort which nothing but gold dust could
> manure, I have but half a liking to the blossom . . ."

Nearly every important scene in the development of the
passion of Rochester and Jane Eyre takes place among trees
—in an orchard, an arbor, a woods, a "leafy enclosure."
When Jane returns from her visit to Gateshead, she finds
Rochester seated among roses, beside "a tall briar, shooting
leafy and flowery branches across the path," and shortly after, their first embrace and his proposal of marriage take
place among "trees laden with ripening fruit," near a blossoming chestnut tree. But the proposal is in fact bigamous,
and if Jane does not know that, nature seems to:

> But what had befallen the night? The moon was not yet set,
> and we were all in shadow: I could scarcely see my master's
> face, near as I was. And what ailed the chestnut tree? it
> writhed and groaned; while wind roared in the laurel walk,
> and came sweeping over us.

Next morning Jane learns that "the great horse-chestnut at
the bottom of the orchard had been struck by lightning in
the night, and half of it split away."

Just before the fatal marriage ceremony, Jane goes to the
orchard and enacts a scene that is preparatory to the end of
the novel:

> . . . I faced the wreck of the chestnut-tree; it stood up, black
> and riven: the trunk, split down the centre, gaped ghastly.
> The cloven halves were not broken from each other, for the
> firm base and strong roots kept them unsundered below;

though community of vitality was destroyed—the sap could flow no more: their great boughs on each side were dead, and next winter's tempests would be sure to fell one or both to earth: as yet, however, they might be said to form one tree — a ruin, but an entire ruin.

"You did right to hold fast to each other," I said: as if the monster-splinters were living things, and could hear me. "I think, scathed as you look, and charred and scorched, there must be a little sense of life in you yet: rising out of that adhesion at the faithful, honest roots: you will never have green leaves more—never more see birds making nests and singing idylls in your boughs; the time of pleasure and love is over with you: but you are not desolate: each of you has a comrade to sympathise with him in his decay." As I looked up at them, the moon appeared momentarily in that part of the sky which filled their fissure; her disk was blood-red, and half-overcast; she seemed to throw on me one bewildered, dreary glance, and buried herself again instantly in the deep drift of cloud. The wind fell, for a second, round Thornfield; but far away over wood and water, poured a wild, melancholy wail: it was sad to listen to, and I ran off again.

When the marriage is halted, it is as if a "Christmas frost had come at midsummer . . . the woods which twelve hours since waved leafy and fragrant as groves between the tropics, now spread, waste, wild and white as pine-forests in wintry Norway. My hopes were all dead . . ."

During the unsatisfactory period at Moor House and Morton, trees and vegetation both tend to disappear, but when Jane at last seeks out the wounded Rochester, the arboreal imagery again becomes prominent. Ferndean, his house, is "deep buried in a wood,"

. . . thick and dark grew the timber of the gloomy wood about it . . . the twilight of close-ranked trees. There was a grass-grown track descending the forest aisle, between hoar and knotty shafts and under branched arches. . . . all was interwoven stem, columnar trunk, dense, summer foliage—no opening anywhere. . . . at last my way opened, the trees thinned a little . . . the house—scarce, by this dim light, distinguishable from the trees . . . "Can there be life here?" I asked. Yes: life of some kind there was; for I heard a movement . . .

Blinded Rochester emerges, and he gropes for the trees with his sound arm. After their reunion, the whole import of this imagery is made explicit:

"I am no better than the old lightning-struck chestnut-tree in Thornfield orchard," he remarked, ere long. "And what right would that ruin have to bid a budding woodbine cover its decay with freshness?"

"You are no ruin, sir—no lightning-struck tree: you are green and vigorous. Plants will grow about your roots, whether you ask them or not, because they take delight in your bountiful shadow; and as they grow they will lean towards you, and wind round you, because your strength offers them so safe a prop.". . .

. . . his old impetuosity was rising. "We must become one flesh without any delay, Jane . . ."

At last, "We entered the wood, and wended homeward." And the next, famous sentence: "Reader, I married him."

We have perhaps labored this documentation of a single, but major strand of imagery in *Jane Eyre* to suggest that its basic organizing principle is like that of dramatic poetry rather than like that of conventionally realistic fiction. From this poetic strain comes its visionary quality and its sustained tone of agitation and excitement. In a realistic novel, much of the action would be intolerable, but in *Jane Eyre*, as it is written, the tone gives it all a visionary coherence and reality.

The Symbolism of Fire and Water in *Jane Eyre*

Eric Solomon

In his analysis of *Jane Eyre*, Eric Solomon identifies "a hard coherence of thematic and symbolic pattern." Specifically, the pervasive images of fire and water serve as a substructure for the entire novel and support the novel's main theme, that Jane must find a middle ground between the "fire" of passion and the "water" of reason and restraint. In addition to the following critical analysis, published in *College English*, Solomon has written articles on numerous novelists and their fiction.

As Mark Schorer has eloquently said, criticism of fiction "must begin with the base of language, with the word, with figurative structures, with rhetoric as skeleton and style as body of meaning." A proper understanding of Charlotte Brontë's achievement in *Jane Eyre* should be based on the symbolic form of the novel. While any perceptive reading of the book must grant the author's artistic excesses—the improbabilities, the stilted dialogue, the lack of restraint, the flat secondary characters—still, the argument for *Jane Eyre*'s continuing fascination must go beyond the usual commonplaces about Charlotte Brontë's forcefulness, her powerful imagination, the vitality of her passionate heroine. I would argue that *Jane Eyre* is not formless "romantic" art. The novel makes up for a certain flabbiness of plot by a hard coherence of thematic and symbolic pattern.

Basically, the novel is divided into four acts and a brief conclusion. In each act the same scenes are played out: Jane comes into conflict with authority, defeats it by her inner strength, and departs into exile. The first act takes place at Gateshead: Aunt Reed is the harsh oppresser; Jane resists unjust punishment and is exiled to Lowood Institution. In

Reprinted from Eric Solomon, "*Jane Eyre:* Fire and Water," *College English*, vol. 25 (1964). (Footnotes in the original have been omitted in this reprint.)

this first section Jane's powerful passion defeats the outside force of Aunt Reed's brutality. Next, at Lowood, Jane learns from her saintly spiritual adviser, Helen Burns, how to overcome the evil cruelty of Mr. Brocklehurst by quiet submission. Thus at Lowood, self-control defeats the inside force of Jane's own passion. When she exiles herself from Lowood and goes to meet her romantic fate at Thornfield, she has formed the two opposing methods of fighting injustice—by aggression and by submission—that will continue to battle within her mind. The basic scene is re-enacted, in a double-edged form, at both Thornfield and Marsh End. Jane gains Rochester's love and defeats Blanche Ingram's upper-class claims by strong submissiveness. Conversely, Jane manages to evade Rochester's authoritarian claims for her body and soul by her quiet aggressiveness. Her indomitable reply "*I* care for myself" repeats the lesson forced upon her by Aunt Reed. Jane's advice to Rochester, "trust in God and yourself," reflects Helen's teaching. As did the first two short acts, this long crucial act ends with Jane's exile—this time into utter isolation, but, as always, she retains her integrity after duty defeats temptation. Once again, at Marsh End, the doughty Jane wins a victory, now over the rigid, evangelical religiosity of St. John Rivers. If Rochester offered love without marriage, Rivers, in a proposal scene that parallels the one in the earlier section, offers marriage without love. As before, Jane saves her identity: "I should still have my unblighted self to turn to. . . ." Jane initially saved herself by submitting to the orders of Rivers and becoming a teacher; she finally saves herself by combatting his domineering spirit that would crush her. Again she escapes, but this time back to Rochester at Ferndean, a chastened, symbolically emasculated Rochester, to whom she pretends to submit (in the guise of a servant) but whom she actually has conquered.

OTHER STRUCTURAL DEVICES

Charlotte Brontë uses other structural methods to make her supposedly rambling novel cohere. There are parallel scenes—Jane's isolation in the red room and, later, in the room with the wounded Mason, for example; or the attempted seductions by Rochester and Rivers. The novel also sets contrasts of character—Rochester and Rivers are opposites, as are Blanche and Rosamund, the Reed sisters and the Rivers sisters. There is considerable foreshadowing: Rochester must lean on Jane when he first meets her and when they come together at the end. The book has a general thematic unity; as the hymn at the start of the novel indicates and as Helen's death makes clear, a motif is the orphan Jane's search for a home (a motif basic to Victorian fiction). By stressing the tensions in each section of the novel between spirit and flesh, order and emotion, submission and revolt, restraint and excitement, conscience and passion, and, finally, love and sin, Charlotte Brontë brings her heroine through a series of temptations, each one starting in isolation and ending in a triumph of integrity.

Much of the imagery of *Jane Eyre* is obvious—the chestnut tree, the grim landscapes, the red room that is like Hell. But two images are so pervasive that they serve as a substructure for the entire novel: fire and water—and their extremes, the flames of lust and the ice of indifference. The fire is in Jane's spirit and in Rochester's eyes. Jane desires "life, fire, feeling"; Rochester has "strange fire in his look." If these two are fire, St. John Rivers (note the last name) contains the icy waters that would put out fire, destroy passion. His nature is frozen over with an "ice of reserve"; when he tells Jane, "I am cold: no fervour infects me," her reply is, "Whereas I am hot, and fire dissolves ice."

FIRE AND WATER

From the start of the novel, Charlotte Brontë's fire and water imagery indicates the essential idea. The fiery passion of Jane, and, later, Rochester must be quenched by the cold waters of self-control—but not destroyed by the ice of repression. If their bodies burn, their minds must dampen the fires. Jane warns herself that secret love might "kindle" within her life an "*ignis fatuus*" [deceptive hope]. Yet it is Rochester who is all-fire: when, disguised as a gypsy, he has his interview with Jane, she feels his powerful attraction and says, "Don't keep me long; the fire scorches me." Rochester, for his part, realizes Jane's double quality; she has the fire of bodily love, "The flame flickers in the eye," but also the cool control of the soul, "the eye shines like dew." Earlier, Rochester insists that Jane is cold because she is alone: "no contact strikes the fire from you that is within you."

When Bertha, Rochester's old passionate flame, sets his bed on fire, Jane saves him by dousing the bed with water.

Miss Brontë's imagery is precise and explains the relationship between the central characters. Bertha represents the flames of hellfire that have already scorched Rochester. Jane, fiery though she is, has sufficient control to water down these fires. Jane "brought my own water jug, baptized the couch afresh, and, by God's aid, succeeded in extinguishing the flames which were devouring it." She will save them both from hellfire by refusing the passionate advances of Rochester. After she learns of his previous marriage, she finally gains release from her burning agony and imagines herself laid down in the dried-up bed of a great river, and "I heard a flood loosened in remote mountains, and felt the torrent come . . . ." Religion—true religion, not the frigid religion that will characterize Rivers—is described in terms of water: "'the waters came into my soul . . . I came into deep waters; the floods overflowed me'." And this water in Jane's spirit enables her to withstand what Rochester calls the "pure, powerful flame" that fuses them. Despite the "hand of fiery iron [that] grasped my vitals," despite her "veins running fire," despite Rochester's "flaming glance" which is likened to the "glow of a furnace," Jane flees to the "wet turf" and sheds "stormy, scalding, heart-wrung tears."

Although Jane is soaked with rain in her wanderings, her emotional fires still burn, ready to be re-awakened when the dangers of Rochester's appeals have passed. Rochester alone must be purged by the fires he long ago lit between himself and Bertha. This time there is no Jane to keep him from the searing, mutilating flames that destroy Bertha and Thornfield, and, ironically, put out the fiery gleam in his eyes. But Jane, meanwhile, is guarding her own flame from the freezing heartlessness of St. John Rivers. His "ice kisses" cannot reach her. She cannot forever "keep the fires of my nature continually low, to compel it to burn inwardly and never utter a cry, though the imprisoned flame consumed vital after vital." She escapes from Rivers' chilling grasp and returns to the scorched ruin of Rochester where she can "kindle the lustre" of his "lamp" which has been "quenched." Soon she re-awakens the glow of their love, and their two natures join in a steady flame that burns neither as wildly as the lightning that destroyed the chestnut, nor as dimly as the setting sun of St. John Rivers' religious dream. The fire-water image underscores the basic idea of *Jane Eyre:* just as love must find a middle way between the flames of passion and the waters of pure reason, so Jane must find a golden mean between egocentric rage and Christlike submission, between Aunt Reed and Helen Burns, between the wild, Byronic Rochester and the tempered, controlled Rivers. Jane Eyre achieves this successful median in her own character and in her future life with the chastened Rochester. Image and idea join in a novel that not only shows the wildly passionate appeal of romantic art but also operates under the concept of formal control.

Jane's Five Homes

Felicia Gordon

In her book *A Preface to the Brontës*, Felicia Gordon
suggests that Jane's five homes serve as structural
devices that mark important stages in Jane's emotional and spiritual development: Jane's pilgrimage
begins at Gateshead, where she rebels against a
cold and unfeeling mother figure. At Lowood, Jane
stands up to the morally bereft Mr. Brocklehurst before finding romantic love at Thornfield, her third
home. When events conspire that cause Jane to flee
to Marsh End, Jane achieves independence and preserves her moral integrity. Finally, at her fifth home,
the newly liberated Jane chooses a loving union
with Rochester.

Jane Eyre functions on one level as a *Bildungsroman* or education novel. The heroine's education takes place in five
stages, corresponding with five houses; Gateshead, Lowood,
Thornfield, Moor House and Ferndean. Each stage of development is overseen by a dominant patriarchal male figure
and each home is experienced as an enclosed world from
which Jane must break out as, in each case, the promise of
protection gives way to the desire for growth and liberty.
Jane, an orphan, may be seen as engaged in a quest for her
real home. But her story is not a simple progression. She
does not merely move from stage to stage as on a chess
board, she can also be thought of as oscillating between Romantic feeling and Christian duty and reason.

GATESHEAD

Jane's education or moral progress is closely linked to the
dynamics of Bunyan's *Pilgrim's Progress*, a book universally
read in the nineteenth century. The novel falls within the
tradition of religious, didactic works, which show a soul
struggling between good and evil forces before arriving at

the heavenly kingdom: 'I seek an Inheritance incorruptible, undefiled and that fadeth not away' (*Pilgrim's Progress*, Part I). But Jane, unlike Bunyan's Christian, seeks her kingdom in this world, without being elevated into an allegorical or universal figure of passion and reason in revolt. She engages in a quest, for love, justice and legitimate authority. Both are lacking at Gateshead, her Aunt Reed's house, where the novel opens; here the Reed children, especially John, torment and humiliate Jane, the outsider. Jane thinks of herself as a child who cannot please other people or inspire love. The novel focuses on the importance of the child's self-definition for the formation of her adult mind. Jane is torn between the conviction of her incapacity to please and a sense of her legitimate worth. 'I was a discord in Gateshead Hall; I was like nobody there.' It is significant that at Gateshead Jane effects her first escape from an oppressive reality through the medium of Romantic art, in her reading of Bewick's *British Birds*. Though the importance accorded to childhood in the novel is Wordsworthian, there is no sentimentality about children. Jane, with whom the reader certainly sympathizes, is not a picture of innocence and charm. The opening scene shows young children squabbling with a sort of casual brutality. The description of the poisonous Reed children probably owes a good deal to the Brontës' experiences as governesses in wealthy families. John Reed even strikes Jane, in a display of arbitrary power, clearly based not only on the fact that he is bigger, and a boy, but on class and money. 'You ought to beg', he taunts, 'and not live here with gentlemen's children like us.'

Mr Reed, who initially gave Jane a home, represents the legitimate authority of the house. Yet Mr Reed is equally a figure of dread; brooding on him when locked in the Red Room, Jane 'sees' his ghost and gives way to nervous terrors. In the context of the novel's theme of spiritual progress, this scene may be interpreted as the equivalent of a trance, the Romantic path to transcendence. Nevertheless, the story remains within the limits of the probable. Bessie, the family nurse, provides an account of what Jane claims to have seen. 'Something passed her, all dressed in white and vanished'— 'a great black dog behind him'—'Three loud raps on the chamber door'—'a light in the churchyard just over his grave.' Although Jane's ghostly vision is accounted for naturalistically, as the overwrought imagination of a sensitive child, the atmosphere of the supernatural is established early in the novel. Mr Reed represents Jane's belief in a kindly father figure who, if he were alive, would shelter and love her; he is in short, a loving God or patriarch, but absent:

> I thought Mr Reed's spirit, harassed by the wrongs of his sister's child, might quit its abode—whether in the church vault or in the unknown world of the departed—and rise before me in this chamber. I wiped my tears and hushed my sobs, fearful lest any sign of violent grief might waken a preternatural voice to comfort me, or elicit from the gloom some haloed face, bending over me in strange pity.

Gateshead, lacking its legitimate master and ruled by the cold, unmotherly Mrs Reed, who in turn is bullied by her son, John, is no real home.

Jane, of course, lacks a mother as well as a father; the maternal figures in the novel are revealing. Jane's aunt, Mrs Reed, recalls the archetypal wicked stepmother. Bessie, the nurse, though kind-hearted, does not treat Jane with any particular favouritism. Miss Temple, at Lowood, succours and consoles her, but her care is limited to what is credible in a teacher. Mrs Fairfax, at Thornfield, a motherly soul if there ever was one, is to Jane's increasingly independent and adventurous mind, good but dull. Given their family circumstances, there is nothing surprising in the fact that the Brontës' novels, generally, lack sympathetic mother figures. In *Jane Eyre* it is nature which functions in the restorative and maternal rôle:

> I have no relative but the universal mother, *Nature;* I will seek her breast and ask repose. . . . Nature seemed to me benign and good; I thought she loved me, outcast as I was. . . . To-night, at least, I would be her guest, as I was her child: my mother would lodge me without money and without price.

Mr Brocklehurst, the headmaster of Lowood School, succeeds Mr Reed as the second example of quasi-paternal authority. Jane's first glimpse of him captures the child's view of a terrifying patriarch, a phallic column:

> I looked up at—a black pillar!— such, at least, appeared to me, at first sight, the straight, narrow, sable-clad shape standing erect on the rug; the grim face at the top was like a carved mask, placed above the shaft by way of capital.

Facing up to Mr Brocklehurst, and overcoming his moral blackmail, is Jane's second instinctive act of rebellion, her first being her refusal to submit to John Reed. At Lowood, Mr Brocklehurst unscrupulously employs the language of religion to humiliate his charges. His unctuous speeches betray a fine tinge of sadism:

> I have a Master to serve whose kingdom is not of this world: my mission is to mortify in these girls the lusts of the flesh, to teach them to clothe themselves with shamefacedness and sobriety, not with braided hair and costly apparel; and each of the young persons before us has a string of hair twisted in plaits which vanity itself might have woven: these, I repeat, must be cut off.

Mr Brocklehurst is a debased parental figure, his authority little more than sexual tyranny. The symbolic meaning of wishing to cut off the girls' hair, cropping their one ornament to curtail their sexual nature, is evident. Intellectually if not emotionally, it is relatively easy for Jane to see through the 'black pillar'. And in spite of her first ominous meeting with Mr Brocklehurst at Gateshead (whose opening conversational gambit is to ask Jane whether she knows where the wicked go after death), Jane looks forward to Lowood as freeing her from the tyranny of her Reed cousins. We notice that, whereas in *Pilgrim's Progress* characters are unambiguous, according entirely with their allegorical titles, Mr Brocklehurst, a clergyman, who allegorically would function as a good man, is intuitively perceived by Jane to be the reverse. Her instinctive knowledge, a Romantic quality, remains an important marker, even when she has gained far greater worldly knowledge.

LOWOOD

Lowood School for all its horrors, is, in many respects, preferable to Jane's first home. So much emphasis has been placed on the historical basis for Lowood (Cowan Bridge) and the identification of the sanctimonious Brocklehurst with the Reverend Carus Wilson, that we risk forgetting that Lowood is also portrayed positively. Mr Brocklehurst's Evangelical reign of terror is mitigated to a great extent by Miss Temple's mildness and reasonableness. At Lowood, Jane finds two moral guides, who have a profound effect on her development. Miss Temple, the headmistress, teaches Jane self-control; Helen Burns, the friend who dies, holds up a model of resignation and forgiveness. Helen is like Bunyan's Faithful, who goes before, to show us the way. Yet another important aspect of Lowood is that in this unprepossessing environment, Jane discovers that she loves study. Her intellectual enthusiasms make even the inadequate food of Lowood irrelevant. 'I would not now have exchanged Lowood with all its privations for Gateshead and its daily luxuries.'

Jane spends ten years at Lowood, under the benign discipline of Miss Temple. After the latter's marriage, however, Jane finds that a transformation has taken place within herself:

> I imagined myself only to be regretting my loss, and thinking how to repair it; but when my reflections were concluded, and I looked up and found that the afternoon was gone, and evening far advanced, another discovery dawned on me— namely, that in the interval I had undergone a transforming process; that my mind had put off all it had borrowed of Miss Temple—or rather, that she had taken with her the serene atmosphere I had been breathing in her vicinity—and that now I was left in my natural element, and beginning to feel the stirring of old emotions. It did not seem as if a prop were withdrawn, but rather as if a motive had gone: it was not the power to be tranquil which had failed me, but the reason for tranquillity was no more. My world had for some years been in Lowood: my experience had been of its rules and systems; now I remembered that the real world was wide, and that a varied field of hopes and fears, of sensations and excitements, awaited those who had courage to go forth into its expanse, to seek real knowledge amidst its perils.

Her decision to leave Lowood is motivated by a desire to 'seek real knowledge of life amidst its perils'. She sets forth on her pilgrimage again, by advertising for a post as governess and receives a favourable reply from a Mrs Fairfax at Thornfield.

THORNFIELD

Thus Jane goes to her third 'home' with a profound desire for change; even a new servitude, she feels, is better than a life of inaction. But Thornfield, too, is little more than a peaceful backwater until transformed by the arrival of Mr Rochester. At Thornfield she discovers Romantic passion, something quite foreign to her experience hitherto. Whereas Jane had rebelled against authority at Gateshead, saying of John Reed, 'Master! How is he my master? Am I a servant?', she willingly calls Mr Rochester master and accepts peremptory treatment from him. Jane enjoys Rochester's eccentric manners, a mixture of frankness and authoritarian command. With Rochester, Jane too, is frank. To Rochester's leading question, 'Do you think me handsome?' she replies with an abrupt, indeed tactless, 'No, sir!' Like Jane, Mr Rochester is unconventional in both manners and looks. So entirely do Thornfield and its owner appear to be the home and master for which Jane had always longed, that the discovery of his bigamous intentions and her decision to flee represent an emotional uprooting, as much as a disappointment in love. As Jane declares to Rochester, 'Wherever you are is my home—my only home.'

The problem of mastery, which tormented Jane as a child at Gateshead, is relevant here. On the one hand, she yearns for authority, a master, a legitimizing and caring principle; on the other, authority proves to be arbitrary, unreliable or tyrannical (Mr Brocklehurst, Mrs Reed, John Reed, Mr Rochester, St John Rivers). Though Jane feels her physical inferiority, she is also convinced of her intellectual capacities and spiritual worth. The moral law to which she appeals when she leaves Rochester is not merely a question of obedience to God. By following, no matter how painfully, her inner promptings of conscience, she can attain self-respect and integrity:

> *I* care for myself. The more solitary, the more friendless, the more unstained I am, the more I will respect myself. I will keep the law given by God; sanctioned by man. I will hold to the principles received by me when I was sane, and not mad—as I am now.

Immediately after her trial of strength with Mr Rochester, when he pleads with her to live with him as his mistress, Jane has a dream, which resembles one of her own eerie paintings:

> then, not a moon, but a white human form shone in the azure, inclining a glorious brow eastward. It gazed and gazed on me. It spoke to my spirit. . . . 'My daughter, flee temptation.' 'Mother, I will.' So I answered after I had waked from the trance-like dream.

The border between dream, trance and reality are deliberately blurred, as when Jane hears Rochester calling her at Moor House. But here her unknown mother speaks to re-establish moral authority over the wavering Jane. She is, then, able to defy the third patriarchal authority whom she loves, rather than fears. And like Bunyan's Pilgrim, she sets out on the next stage of her journey, 'a new Road; one I had never travelled'.

MARSH END

Though the element of coincidence strains the patience of some readers, the novel's quest or romance element can be thought to legitimize the discovery of Marsh End and Moor House as Jane's fourth home where she finds blood relations. At Marsh End, Jane discovers the same grouping of siblings as at Gateshead, including herself, three girls and a boy (the same arrangement, of course, as that in the Brontë family). But here the Rivers family represents an ideal of development, instead of the miserable, thwarted, vain and self-indulgent life of the Reed household. Before arriving at this earthly ideal, Jane undergoes severe physical trials of hunger and cold and is forced to beg for food, finally eating burnt porridge destined for pigs. . . .

With the Rivers sisters, Jane enjoys a relationship of mutual respect, where all labour to educate themselves and to help one another. Authority only intervenes in the figure of their brother, St John Rivers, perhaps the most threatening and fascinating of the novel's male figures. His Evangelical enthusiasm and integrity, combined with a fine intellect and physical beauty, make him a redoubtable antagonist. How can Jane refuse his appeal to join in God's work and purpose, which he is so certain that he incarnates?

> I listen to my duty, and keep steadily in view my first aim—to do all things to the glory of God. My Master was long-suffering; so will I be. I cannot give you up to perdition as a vessel of wrath: repent—resolve, while there is yet time. Remember, we are bid to work while it is day—warned that 'the night cometh when no man shall work'. . . . God give you strength to choose the better part which shall not be taken from you. . . .

In effect, St John Rivers offers Jane a chance to follow a reliable moral and spiritual guide. What she understands, in spite of her veneration for his calling, is the arrogance of his belief that he is God's interpreter. Applying what he believes is God's purpose to himself is one thing; to impose his law on another person has a flavour of tyranny about it. The power of the religious patriarch satirized in Mr Brocklehurst genuinely terrifies Jane in Rivers, because both her duty and her religious belief seem to urge her to follow him.

A conventional Romantic or Gothic novel would have seen in St John Rivers the answer to a maiden's prayer. Mr Rochester, the Gothic villain, would have given way to the stainless Gothic hero. We notice that in *Jane Eyre* and *Villette* Charlotte allows her heroine (unusually for the conventions of the day) to consider seriously loving two suitors. Apropos of *Villette*, Thackeray sneered at 'the author's naive confes-

sion of being in love with two men at the same time' (letter
to Lucy Baxter, 11 March 1853). Since St John Rivers is both
morally superior to Rochester and far more handsome, his
rejection by Jane is particularly remarkable. She recognizes
that Rivers' sense of mission requires a massive egotism that
leaves no room for anyone else. Jane knows she will be
crushed by him. Rivers is as much a tyrant in his way as
John Reed. He is a subtle, intelligent and entirely sincere
Brocklehurst. Though Jane can contemplate serving him as
a missionary in India, she cannot bear the notion of marrying him without love. 'Can I receive from him the bridal
ring, endure all the forms of love . . . and know that the spirit
is absent?'

FERNDEAN

Jane's final home or resting place, Ferndean, lies in the
heart of a forest, a Romantic labyrinth, which like the similar image in Dante implies the doubts and difficulties surrounding her quest for Rochester:

> I looked round in search of another road. There was none: all
> was interwoven stem, columnar trunk, dense summer fo-
> liage—no opening anywhere.

Moor House, by contrast, where Jane found her independence, is set in bracing hilly country. Ferndean, its physical
antithesis, shrouded in a deep wood, is a shelter from the
world. Perhaps the least satisfying aspect of the novel's
happy ending is that the marriage with Rochester is depicted
as a relationship of almost suffocating harmony, prefigured
by the environment. Certainly the dense wood, the close vegetation, is a favourite Romantic image, and symbolizes
Jane's safe return to her Romantic self, though with the
sanction of reason and duty.

The five 'homes' in *Jane Eyre*, as a structural and thematic
device, mark clear stages in Jane's development. From her
turbulent and loveless childhood, she goes in quest of justice, love and religious consolation. True and false guides
lead her: Miss Temple, Helen Burns, Mr Brocklehurst, and
Rochester himself, who can be both false and true. Jane's rejection of St John Rivers is an acknowledgement that she
must be her own guide; that her strength is in herself. She is
then free to help Rochester. The novel's conclusion suggests
that there is no authority save one's own integrity founded
on religious principle. The theme of religion fittingly closes

the novel. St John Rivers' single-minded dedication to God, though inhuman in its intensity, remains a troubling instance of the human desire to transcend the world. He is compared to Bunyan's Greatheart, 'who guards his pilgrim convoy from the onslaught of Apollyon.' Jane, however, chooses the world of flesh and blood. Ferndean attains an Edenic status, as is clear from the Miltonic echo at the close of Chapter 37, reversing, as it were, the expulsion from Paradise. Whereas Milton's Adam and Eve 'through Eden took their solitary way' into the world of sin and death, Charlotte's closes her chapter with the sentence: 'We entered the wood and wended homeward.' The novel's quest is as much for the true home as for romantic love.

Prophetic Visions: The Three Pictures

Thomas Langford

The significance of Jane's three pictures has been the subject of much critical analysis. In Thomas Langford's assessment, each picture—as a symbolic representation of the major stages of Jane's life— provides structure and unity to the novel. The first picture symbolizes the spiritual isolation and disappointment of Jane's early life at Lowood. The final two pictures foreshadow events to come: The second prophesies romatic love at Thornfield and the third suggests the cold asceticism and lack of love Jane will experience at Marsh End. Thomas Langford of Texas Technological College in Lubbock, Texas, contributed the following critical analysis to the *Victorian Newsletter*.

One of the enigmas in Charlotte Brontë's first published novel has been the description of the three pictures in Chapter Thirteen. The three are isolated from a larger number of sketches that Jane presents and are scrutinized closely by Rochester. "'While he is so occupied," Jane describes the pictures for the reader. She points out that their conception surpassed their execution, that each was "but a pale portrait of the thing I had conceived." There are sufficient hints to cause the perceptive reader to believe that the pictures she attempted to produce were parts of a kind of prophetic vision. She says that she "saw them with the spiritual eye," and Rochester says, after viewing them, "you have secured the shadow of your thought; but no more." He suggests further that parts of the pictures are strange, such that she "must have seen in a dream."

With these clues, it is not illogical to assume that the pictures may represent the three major sections of Jane's life. It is generally conceded, I think, that the novel falls rather natu-

Reprinted from Thomas Langford, "The Three Pictures in *Jane Eyre*," *The Victorian Newsletter*, Spring 1967, by permission of the author.

rally into three parts—the Lowood, Thornfield, and Marsh End sections—each of which represents a major stage in the life and character development of Jane Eyre. If the three pictures are prophetic visions (and surely this is as acceptable and appropriate as the telepathic call Jane receives from Rochester toward the end of the novel), then it may be expected that they will rather effectively symbolize the dominant themes of each major part of the book (and of Jane's life).

JANE'S BLEAK CHILDHOOD

Following this thesis, we can observe that the first picture presents an accurate symbolical portrayal of Jane's childhood and adolescence. The image is one of spiritual isolation and disappointment. The "swollen sea" with its turbulent billows and "clouds low and livid" accurately characterize Jane's traumatic existence in the Reed household and most of the aspects of her Lowood life. The "one gleam of light" seems to suggest the friendship of Helen Burns, but even this light reveals also the short-lived nature of this friendship, for visible in it are the mast-perched cormorant and the submerged corpse, symbols of the forces of evil and the end of friendship at Helen's death. The bracelet, set with gems painted in tints as "brilliant" and "glittering" as "pallette could yield," represents the brightness of the single happiness Jane had known in this friendship. The cormorant holds the bracelet in its beak, suggesting the evil force that consumed the life of Helen Burns.

PASSIONATE LOVE

The second picture is clearly a vision of the goddess of love and is connected in various ways with Thornfield. It is in this section of the novel that Jane feels most strongly her womanly instincts and is awakened to the exalting powers of a transcendent love. Of the three pictures, only this one is specifically discussed by Rochester; this is the prophecy that concerns him. The visionary quality of the picture is enhanced by his recognition and identification of Latmos, a hill he is familiar with but which Jane cannot have seen except in a dream. The twilight sky, suffused moonlight, and tints "dusk and soft" increase the effective suggestiveness of this Venus vision. The eyes shining "dark and wild," the hair streaming "'shadowy, like a beamless cloud torn by storm or by electric travail,'" all suggest the stormy nature of the Rochester relationship and the violent separation at the end of the section.

ASCETIC AUSTERITY

The final picture is the opposite of everything in the second. Where the other reveals the warmth and passion of love, this last is the embodiment of ascetic austerity. This picture foretells Jane's experience with the cold crusader, St. John Rivers. He is not the "iceberg," or even the "colossal head" resting on it; these things represent rather the bloodless, barren, living death of the experience he tempts Jane toward. The words of this picture's description are carefully chosen; "pinnacle," "iceberg," "polar winter sky," and "northern lights" all evoke just that degree of heightened frigid saintliness that St. John stands for in the novel. The "colossal head" is death itself. Its "sable veil," "brow quite bloodless, white as bone," and "eye hollow and fixed, blank of meaning but for the glassiness of despair," coldly and accurately portray the spiritual (if not the physical) death to-

PAST OR FUTURE MINDSCAPES?

In the following excerpt, critic M.B. McLaughlin counters Thomas Langford's view that Jane's pictures are prophetic. McLaughlin contends instead that the pictures represent past—not future—experiences.

[Thomas Langford] maintains that the pictures are not only prophetic but help provide unity for the novel. But when he attempts specificity in interpreting the pictures, his straining is obvious. His assignment of symbols becomes clearly arbitrary, as when he suggests that the bracelet torn from the corpse's arm in the first picture represents Jane's broken relationship with Helen Burns. But it is possible, I believe, to see this picture and the other two as imaginative representations of real and traumatic *past* experiences with a less arbitrary interpretation of symbols.

It is the death of Mr. Reed that has made Jane's early life so miserable, the broken relationship with him that has made her so vulnerable. One of the most vivid scenes of Jane's childhood is that of her imprisonment in the Red Room. Here, too, she is preoccupied with death, and hears "the rushing of wings.". . . In the Red Room experience there is "a gleam from a lantern" as there is "one gleam of light" in the first picture.

The second picture, which Langford calls "clearly a vision of the goddess of love and connected in various ways with

ward which Jane is tempted by St. John's proposal of a marriage without love and a missionary service without dedication.

If there is yet any doubt as to the meaning of this picture, it should be settled by a positive identification of the head and of the "ring of white flame" that encircles it as a double-duty halo and crown, both emblems of the saint and martyr. They are not such emblems for Jane, however; to her they spell death. The lines she quotes, "The likeness of a Kingly Crown," and "the shape which shape had none," are from Milton's description of Death in *Paradise Lost*, Book II.

This fact brings us back to an earlier figure, attention to which will allow a meaningful conclusion to this interpretation of the three pictures. It seems likely that the cormorant in the first picture was suggested by the cormorant in Book IV of *Paradise Lost*. The quotation of the two lines in the description of the last picture shows that the author was making a quite

Thornfield," can also, I think, be treated in another way. The picture is one of serenity. The image of electric travail is used only as a simile to describe the way in which the "shadowy hair" is separated. The eyes that "shone dark and wild" are eyes of spirit—the kind of spirit Miss Temple displays in ordering bread and cheese for the students at Lowood. . . . This second picture can be seen as an idealized portrait of Miss Temple at Lowood. The picture is of a goddess—a "vision of the Evening Star." Venus is the evening star, and Venus, of course, is the goddess of love. Miss Temple furnishes Jane with affection, love, and concern at an extremely impressionable time in Jane's life. Both pictures tell, then, of a traumatic loss and abandonment—the first symbolizing the consequences of Mr. Reed's death, the second that of Miss Temple's loss through marriage.

The third picture presents more difficulty. Certainly it seems prophetic of St. John Rivers, largely because of the images of icebergs and coldness. But St. John Rivers and Mr. Brocklehurst are very much alike in their coldness and aloofness. Jane associates the two men in her mind several times in the novel. The martyr imagery of the third painting can, I think, be related to Helen Burns. And the cold, male image of Mr. Brocklehurst would be contiguously associated with this memory.

M.B. McLaughlin, *Victorian Newsletter*, Spring 1972.

conscious association between certain images in Milton's work and her own. With this evidence of what influences were at work in the author's mind, it would seem that the cormorant perched on the mast must certainly have been suggested by Milton's description of Satan as a cormorant evilly leering from out the branches of the Tree of Life. That earlier bird looked enviously upon the happiness of Adam and Eve in paradise and plotted their downfall through temptation. *Jane Eyre*'s cormorant seems equally envious of Jane's happiness, as symbolized by the bracelet he has snatched in his beak. It is likely that the function of the cormorant in this first picture is to suggest the forces that will seek the downfall of Jane through temptation. And the nature of that temptation is foreshadowed in the second and third pictures.

The second picture, as noted earlier, is the Thornfield period. The moods and figures are those of love and reflect the intense attraction between Jane and Rochester. But the temptation of this section is for Jane to accept the calling of that love against the barriers of convention that are reared at last to oppose it. She successfully withstands this temptation and leaves Thornfield to maintain her standards of right behavior.

In the last picture, there is reflected Jane's temptation to accept a relationship with St. John Rivers that would have met the test of outward convention, but would have destroyed her spirit for lack of love. The cold asceticism of St. John would have meant death for Jane, both spiritually and physically. In the Rochester episode, Jane is tempted to satisfy her love in violation of convention. In this last part she is tempted to enter into a relationship which would satisfy convention but in which there is no love. Both temptations are met and resisted, and Jane retains her integrity, if in loneliness. The last three chapters bring a hasty resolution by revealing conditions that will allow Rochester and Jane to be reunited in a morally and artistically satisfactory situation.

PROPHETIC IMAGES

The pictures are prophecy, with overtones of both *Paradise Lost* and *Paradise Regained*. They embrace in their scope the three major sections of Jane Eyre's life and focus on the three most crucial situations of the novel. This interpretation manifests the intricate nature of the novel's unity, in contrast with the view of some that the work has a rather broken, merely episodic structure.

CHAPTER 2

Jane Eyre's Narrative

READINGS ON
JANE EYRE

First-Person Narration

Earl A. Knies

In *Jane Eyre*, the heroine narrates her own story. Literary critic Earl A. Knies outlines some of the disadvantages traditionally attributed to first-person narration. For example, critics find this form inadequate in portraying the character of the narrator or in describing events that unfold in the narrator's absence. Knies, however, describes how Brontë deftly overcomes these obstacles, ultimately creating a passionate and thoroughly reliable narrative. Knies has published several articles about Charlotte Brontë and is the author of *The Art of Charlotte Brontë*, from which the following critical analysis is excerpted.

[*Jane Eyre*] is potentially absurd, highly improbable, apparently artless—when viewed in plot summary; but the novel is none of these things when it is considered as a total work of art. For Charlotte added more than "startling incident." By choosing to write in the person of a woman, she made it possible for herself to project the passionate involvement in her story that was to become her greatest asset. And her use of a thoroughly realized first-person narrator did more than (as some critics have suggested) provide a superficial unity for an otherwise "artless" construction. The question in a first-person narrative is not whether the actions could happen in the real world but whether they could occur in the world of the narrator's mind. If Jane is real, then her story is real; for the world she describes is the world of her perceptions. The quality of that world, of course, determines the quality of the novel.

AN ADEQUATE METHOD

Critics sometimes question the wisdom of Charlotte's choice of first person to tell her story. Carl Grabo cites *Jane Eyre* as "an ex-

Excerpted from Earl A. Knies, *The Art of Charlotte Brontë*, chap. 4 (Athens: Ohio University Press, 1969). Copyright © 1969 by Earl A. Knies. Reprinted by permission of the author. (Notes in the original have been omitted in this reprint.)

cellent illustration of a novel which struggles with an inadequate method":

> Jane's difficulties in spinning her incidents, in getting the situation of her story before us, are sufficiently obvious. Greater is the difficulty of self-portraiture. She must be perceptive but not too perceptive, must be naive and yet wise, bold yet charming. She must analyze herself enough and not too much. Though Charlotte Brontë succeeds in her attempt, the effort of the struggle is written upon the pages of the book. . . . Had the author written from a different point of view, omniscient of Jane and observant of the other characters, little vividness would be lost and much else would have been gained: swiftness, deftness, and, in the delineation of the heroine, a sharper, more triumphant portrait.

But the matter is less simple than Grabo makes it; he seems not to realize that there is a considerable difference between "I" and "she," that third-person omniscience is a distancing factor that would make the events of the novel truly improbable. Once we got outside of Jane and looked *at* her instead of seeing the world through her eyes, we could no longer be convinced by the Byronism of Rochester or the improbability of mental telepathy or any of the other potential absurdities in the book. If we take any passage in *Jane Eyre* and change the "I" to "she," immediately something is lost, and that something is more than vividness. The end of the first chapter, for example: "Four hands were immediately laid upon me, and I was borne up stairs"; or the end of the twenty-second: "Never had he called me more frequently to his presence; never been kinder to me when there—and, alas! never I loved him so well." It is a point which will be taken up later in more detail.

When we search for the evidences of Charlotte's struggle to get the situation of the story before us, we have difficulty finding them. Weaknesses there are, but they are not the result of an inadequate method. On the other hand, most of the strengths clearly *are* the result of the method. The opening chapter does a masterful job of getting the story going, giving us enough of the basic situation to make the action meaningful but at the same time avoiding extensive exposition. At the end of the chapter we are forcibly drawn into the story as those four sets of hands are laid on Jane—and us, for we have already been compelled to make an emotional commitment. *The Professor* had begun with the awkward letter device and then proceeded in a reasonably strict chronological order from that point onward. *Jane Eyre* plunges immediately into the action of the story without any preliminary flourishes, and, although its development is also chronological, necessary information about events preceding the time of the story is periodically being presented in a thoroughly natural way, for we learn about these events at the same time that Jane does. Thus, although the chronological arrangement keeps the story line perfectly clear and easy to follow, *Jane Eyre* is really a mosaic of bits of the past and the present.

FORWARD-MOVING NARRATIVE

The skill with which these expository passages are blended into the forward motion of the narration is apparent in the following examples. While Jane is lying ill after her terrifying experience in the Red Room, she overhears Bessie and Abbot, the maids, talking about her parents, and she learns "for the first time" the conditions under which she had become an orphan. The revelation does not seem unnatural, however, for it is worked smoothly into the maids' conversation. Bessie is inclined to feel some pity for Jane, but Abbot will have none of it: "... one cannot really care for such a little toad as that." Further information about Jane's background is revealed by Mrs. Reed on her deathbed. She tells how her husband had taken Jane at the death of her parents and how Mrs. Reed had hated her from the first. This bit of exposition is functional in the scene, since it emphasizes the intensity of a hatred that Mrs. Reed is unable to overcome even when death is imminent. She also tells Jane of her Uncle John's visit, earlier hinted at by Bessie when she visited Jane at Lowood. The rest of that subplot is sketched in by St. John Rivers near the end of the book, when he tells of her inheritance. And the background of the Rivers family is given in a conversation with Hannah, the maid, while Jane helps her clean gooseberries.

Jane learns about Rochester partly from Mrs. Fairfax, but largely through his own confessions. That such conversations might seem unnatural must have occurred to Charlotte, for she has Rochester admit that it is strange that he should choose "a quaint, inexperienced girl" to tell "stories of his opera-mistresses to"; yet he feels that she was "made to be the recipient of secrets" and that hers is not the sort of mind "liable to take infection"—and we know her well enough by this time to agree. The full story of Rochester's past, the history of his marriage and subsequent debauchery, is told when it has to be: after Jane's marriage ceremony has been interrupted.

The finest piece of exposition is that which occurs when Jane returns to Thornfield after hearing Rochester's call. She discovers the Hall in ruins, and to learn what happened she goes to the local inn, where the host is perfectly happy to answer her questions but is at the same time unaware of her identity. He therefore replies to her questions with a true innkeeper's expansiveness, telling her not only what she wants to know but also a great deal about herself. Try as she will to keep him on the subject, he continually wanders back to what must have been a subject of great local interest and conjecture—Jane's relationship with Rochester.

> "The discovery was brought about in the strangest way [he says]. There was a young lady, a governess at the Hall, that Mr Rochester fell in—"
>
> "But the fire," I suggested.
>
> "I'm coming to that, ma'am—that Mr Edward fell in love with. The servants say that they never saw anybody so much in love as he was: he was after her continually. They used to watch him—servants will, you know, ma'am—and he set store on her past everything: for all, nobody but him thought her so very handsome. She was a small thing, they say, almost like a child. I never saw her myself; but I've heard Leah, the housemaid, tell of her. Leah liked her well enough. Mr Rochester was about forty, and this governess not twenty; and you see, when gentlemen of his age fall in love with girls, they are often like as if they were bewitched: well, he would marry her."
>
> "You shall tell me this part of the story another time," I said. . . .

But on and on he goes in the same agonizing detail, just as any garrulous innkeeper would be likely to do. The scene is brilliant, then, not only for its naturalness, its dramatic irony, and its suspense, but also for its usefulness. For in addition to serving the first three purposes, it reviews key situations from a new perspective. We are given some idea of how the whole affair looked to those who were not a part of it at the same time that some of the related intensity necessarily lost during the Moor House interlude is reestablished.

ATTENDANT DISADVANTAGES

The examples of exposition discussed above illustrate the skill with which Charlotte Brontë conducted her first-person narrative. That skill is even more apparent when we consider some of the other difficulties traditionally attributed to first-person narration. Some of these "attendant disadvantages," as Clayton Hamilton calls them, are "that it is often difficult to account for the hero's presence in every scene, that he cannot be an eyewitness to events happening at the same time in different places, and that it is hard to account for his possession of knowledge regarding those details of the plot which have no immediate bearing on himself." None of these difficulties are apparent in *Jane Eyre*. There simply are no details of plot which do not have an immediate bearing on Jane; the only things that *are* important are the things she knows. She must learn some important things at second hand, but the manner of their presentation is perfectly natural. Because she presents exposition dramatically—through scene rather than through summary— we are present when Rochester tells about his past, when the innkeeper tells about the burning of Thornfield—and so everything seems to be happening within Jane's consciousness even though the events took place when Jane was not actually present. And certainly there is no problem in explaining her presence in every scene that she reports.

JANE'S SELF-PORTRAIT

The real triumph of *Jane Eyre*, as almost every commentator on the book has noted, is, of course, the character of Jane. Yet Grabo is not alone in his feeling that first-person narration creates difficulty in character portrayal. Others also comment on its inability to make a deep study of the central character. Hamilton notes the inadequacy of first person to deal with "a story in which the main events are mental or subjective. We can hardly imagine George Eliot writing in the first person: 'the psychological novel' demands the third." Percy Lubbock agrees in part: ". . . when the man in the book is expected to make a picture of himself, a searching and elaborate portrait, then the limit of his capacity is touched and passed; or rather there is a better method" and that is, for him, the method of James, which Grabo advocates.

Why can't the narrator make an elaborate portrait of himself? "All means of direct delineation are taken from him," says Hamilton. "He cannot write essays on his merits or faults; he can neither describe nor analyze himself; he cannot see himself as others see him. We must derive our sense of who and what he is, solely from the things he does and says, and from his manner of telling us about them." Moreover, the characterization of a first-person protagonist has inherent dangers. Trollope sees two equally distasteful alternatives: "The reader is unconsciously taught to feel that the writer is glorifying himself, and rebels against the self-praise. Or otherwise the 'I' is pretentiously humble, and offends from exactly the other point of view." Esther Summerson is an obvious example of the second type of narrator, and Charlotte Brontë's feeling that she is merely a caricature of an amiable nature has been shared by many readers. What Charlotte is saying, however, is not that Dickens' method is wrong but that his management of it in this instance is faulty.

JANE: AN ADMIRABLE CHARACTER

For within the conventions of first-person narration it is possible to present an admirable character without obvious self-glorification or pretentious humility. Charlotte Brontë's heroines have a particular advantage because they are characters not liked by everyone they meet and because they are plain. The frankness with which these facts are accepted by Jane and Lucy makes us more willing to accept the good things they must tell us about themselves. Moreover, even though a first-person narrator cannot write essays on himself, he can see himself as others see him if he is the kind of person who invites frank comments from other people. Every person in the book helps, to some extent, to characterize Jane, either by direct comment about her or by her reaction to them. Much of her characterization comes through Rochester, who constantly amazes Jane with his ability to read her thoughts. But, as Kathleen Tillotson comments, ". . . we are so much occupied in discovering his own still more mysterious character and attitude that we hardly notice *how* we are being helped to see Jane." And it is not simply what he says about her that helps to characterize her; the things he chooses to tell her about himself also provide a great deal of information. We cannot conceive of his telling Blanche Ingram about his Byronic past any more than we can conceive of her listening without horror or shock.

The interaction among the personages of the novel, then, carries much of the burden of characterization. Even though Jane enlists our sympathy in such a way that we feel about the various characters much as she does, still, we are not forced to accept her feelings simply because they are hers; her friends and foes are presented dramatically, in such a way that we can accept or reject them on the basis of their actions. We do not, for example, dislike Mrs. Reed or Brocklehurst or Blanche Ingram merely because Jane does, but we do dislike them for the same reason that she does: we are repelled by their meanness, their hypocrisy, their pettiness. The elaborate use of foil characters—the Reed sisters and the Rivers sisters, Rochester and St. John, Brocklehurst (the black pillar) and St. John (the marble pillar), Blanche Ingram and Rosamond Oliver, Bessie and Abbot, to name only some of them—also helps to portray the various personalities, and, because they all come into contact with Jane, to portray her.

Of course, Jane does characterize herself through the things she says and does, and her frankness, both in talking to characters within the novel and in talking to us, convinces us of her reliability. We never get the feeling that she is trying to varnish the truth. "You examine me, Miss Eyre," says Rochester; "do you think me handsome?" "No, sir," she blurts out, without pausing to grope for a more conventional and less honest reply. The scene is echoed after the existence of Rochester's mad wife has been revealed. "You know I am a scoundrel, Jane?" he asks wistfully. Her reply is again disturbingly brief and honest: "Yes, sir." Nor does she hesitate to tell us, her "Reader," about feelings that a respectable young girl of the 1840's would be likely to conceal carefully. Watching Rochester mingle with his guests at Thornfield, Jane compares him with them:

> My master's colourless, olive face, square, massive brow, broad and jetty eyebrows, deep eyes, strong features, firm, grim mouth,—all energy, decision, will,—were not beautiful, according to rule; but they were more than beautiful to me: they were full of an interest, an influence that quite mastered me,—that took my feelings from my own power and fettered them in his. I had not intended to love him: the reader knows I had wrought hard to extirpate from my soul the germs of love there detected; and now, at the first renewed view of him, they spontaneously revived, green and strong! He made me love him without looking at me.

It is small wonder that Charlotte's contemporaries found *Jane Eyre* shocking; it is also easy to understand why we believe her.

This complete honesty, this perfect candor, then, provides a structure upon which the reliability of the narrative is built. Once we believe in Jane, we are willing to suspend our disbelief about incidents in the novel which seem improbable.

The Present Tense in *Jane Eyre*

Edgar F. Shannon Jr.

At least seven times in *Jane Eyre*, Charlotte Brontë shifts from the past to the present tense. These deliberate tense changes, according to Edgar F. Shannon Jr., indicate structural divisions in the novel and foreshadow major changes in the story, such as when Jane embarks on her journey to Thornfield. Furthermore, emotionally charged scenes reach the reader in the present tense, evoking the immediacy and drama that Jane herself experiences as events unfold. Edgar F. Shannon Jr., an assistant professor of English at Harvard University, contributed the following essay to *Nineteenth-Century Fiction.*

As everyone will recall, *Jane Eyre* is written in the first person singular, purportedly by the heroine herself, ten years after her marriage to Edward Rochester—the concluding incident of the narrative. As Percy Lubbock indicates in his pioneer study, *The Craft of Fiction* (1921), the autobiographical method precludes the vagaries of an omniscient author, provides a constant point of view, and, through supposed relation by a participant in the action, lends authority and credibility to the tale. But a story told in this manner suffers from the reader's inability to perceive events directly: the narrator stands in the way. The reader must accept an account of what has happened instead of seeing the actors themselves; and the technique reminds him that the action has actually been completed some time before the narration began. Through this displacement in time, the story loses some of its vividness and power of conviction. Yet in *Jane Eyre* Charlotte Brontë reduces the handicap inherent in her method by pertinent shifts from the past to the present tense.

Reprinted from Edgar F. Shannon Jr., "The Present Tense in *Jane Eyre*," *Nineteenth-Century Fiction*, vol. 10 (September 1955), pp. 141–45, by permission. Copyright © 1955 by The Regents of the University of California.

In at least seven passages (the number is of no mystical import), varying in length from twenty lines to almost two pages, the author employs this device to convey either rising emotional tension or a new departure in the story. Describing the evening in the drawing room at Thornfield on the second night of Rochester's house party, for example, she twice hurries the narration forward with the present tense. Skillfully depicting a number of characters simultaneously animated, the technique presents immediately to the reader the brilliancy of the scene as it appears to Jane and evokes the charged atmosphere that compels her self-acknowledgment of love for Rochester, with its concomitant dread of Blanche Ingram's rival charms. Before the novelist slips back into the past tense, the first passage appropriately focuses attention upon Rochester; the second upon Rochester and Blanche. Through the present tense, the reader, rather than being called upon to believe a report of Jane's emotions in the past, experiences them at the moment they arise. Similarly her sensations as she eagerly approaches Thornfield after her absence at Mrs. Reed's sickbed and death and those when Rochester and his cigar trap her in the garden just before she is to hear his unexpected proposal of marriage reach the reader in the present tense. And Miss Brontë also discloses in the present Jane's extended reflections concerning her new duties and past conduct on the evening of her first day as schoolmistress at Morton.

STRUCTURAL DIVISIONS

But the two most significant instances of the present tense in *Jane Eyre* occur at the beginning of chapters xi and xxviii. Chapter xi opens as follows:

> A new chapter in a novel is something like a new scene in a play; and when I draw up the curtain this time, reader, you must fancy you see a room in the George Inn at Millcote, with such large figured papering on the walls as inn rooms have; such a carpet, such furniture, such ornaments on the mantelpiece, such prints; including a portrait of George the Third, and another of the Prince of Wales, and a representation of the death of Wolfe. All this is visible to you by the light of an oil lamp hanging from the ceiling, and by that of an excellent fire, near which I sit in my cloak and bonnet; my muff and umbrella lie on the table, and I am warming away the numbness and chill contracted by sixteen hours' exposure to the rawness of an October day: I left Lowton at four o'clock A.M., and the Millcote town clock is now just striking eight.

Reader, though I look comfortably accommodated, I am not very tranquil in my mind. I thought when the coach stopped here there would be some one to meet me; I looked anxiously round as I descended the wooden steps the "boots" placed for my convenience, expecting to hear my name pronounced, and to see some description of carriage waiting to convey me to Thornfield. Nothing of the sort was visible: and when I asked a waiter if any one had been to inquire after a Miss Eyre, I was answered in the negative: so I had no resource but to request to be shown into a private room: and here I am waiting, while all sorts of doubts and fears are troubling my thoughts.

It is a very strange sensation to inexperienced youth to feel itself quite alone in the world, cut adrift from every connection, uncertain whether the port to which it is bound can be reached, and prevented by many impediments from returning to that it has quitted. The charm of adventure sweetens that sensation, the glow of pride warms it; but then the throb of fear disturbs it; and fear with me became predominant, when half an hour elapsed and still I was alone.

Not only are these paragraphs the beginning of a new chapter; they are the beginning of the second major section of the book. The trials of childhood and of Lowood School contained in the first ten chapters are behind; the young lady is about to make her entrance into the world. Although the author's endeavor to exploit features of the drama is apparent, and her repeated direct address to the "reader" is disturbing to modern ears, she achieves the effect she desires. For the moment, the reader's displacement in time is completely overcome: he hears the clock striking as Jane pauses on the threshold of a new life. Though Thornfield (the overtones of "thorn field" are manifest) is remotely situated, it is a microcosm; and as the comparison with drama suggests, it will be the stage for intensified action and passion. The theater with its audience prefigures the illusory and unreal aspect of Thornfield and the sophistication and worldliness Jane will encounter there. The present tense and the dramatic simile excite the reader's expectancy; and when the lights have dimmed and the curtain rises, the anxious girl waiting under the fading portraits of George the Third, the Prince of Wales, and the dying Wolfe indicates the essential loneliness in which Jane Eyre, like everyone else, must meet the tests of character that society imposes.

Chapter xxviii commences the third and final section of the book; for Jane the drama of Thornfield is over. The first paragraph records the end of her headlong flight from Rochester:

> Two days are passed. It is a summer evening; the coachman has set me down at a place called Whitcross; he could take me no farther for the sum I had given, and I was not possessed of another shilling in the world. The coach is a mile off by this time; I am alone. At this moment I discover that I forgot to take my parcel out of the pocket of the coach, where I had placed it for safety; there it remains, there it must remain; and now, I am absolutely destitute.

Once more the heroine must undertake life anew, and once more the author, by the change of tense, makes the reader feel concurrently with Jane the utter isolation of her plight, as she stands at the symbolic crossroads on a desolate moor, described in the present tense in the succeeding paragraph. Having successfully withstood Rochester's passion, she must now survive the opposite temptation of St. John Rivers' asceticism. The tranquil natural setting for her fresh start that will lead to this last struggle contrasts effectively with the interior of the inn at Millcote and the close atmosphere of a playhouse. (In keeping with the opening of the two sections, Rochester pleads with Jane to become his mistress in the library at Thornfield, while Rivers attempts to will her to marriage in a wild glen.)

THE NATURAL ORDER

The prominence of nature at the outset of the concluding portion of the novel implies the terms in which Jane's predicament will be resolved. The proper equilibrium of all nature—inanimate, human, and divine—must be established for her to attain self-realization. When she strikes into the heath from the crossroads, she derives solace from God's majesty revealed in the stars, and she nestles to sleep, lulled on the breast of "the universal mother, Nature." But nature alone is insufficient to maintain life. After one night Jane must seek sustenance and shelter from mankind; to attempt to depend entirely upon outdoor nature, she recognizes, would itself be unnatural. By fleeing from Rochester and reaffirming God's omnipotence, she has righted an imbalance of the natural order caused by her having put her master above God; by resisting Rivers, she avoids the danger of crushing her innate proclivities, which she realizes would be the result of becoming his missionary helpmeet. With Jane's ordeal completed and with Rochester's disproportionate love chastened by adversity and his pride reduced to humility before God, their marriage is predestined. As she, in her capacity as narrator, had written earlier, "Sympathies, I believe, exist: (for instance, between far-distant, long-absent, wholly estranged relatives; asserting, notwithstanding their alienation, the unity of the source to which each traces his origin) whose workings baffle mortal comprehension. And signs, for aught we know, may be but the sympathies of Nature with man." Sympathy of natures, both elemental and human, transmits the cry of Rochester's heart to Jane's. Whereas storm and lightning had protested Rochester's plan to desecrate order, and fire had consumed the vice and madness of Thornfield, his and Jane's reunion takes place against a benign background of profuse vegetation, and life-giving water bathes Ferndean when she arrives. The name itself, meaning "fern valley" (*dean* from OE *denu*), supplies a benediction connoting shelter and repose.

It is thus through occasional, inconspicuous use of the present tense that Charlotte Brontë not only heightens the immediacy of certain scenes but also marks and foreshadows the structural divisions of the novel.

Jane: A Successful Storyteller

Carol Bock

Reading and storytelling form a central motif in
Jane Eyre, writes Carol Bock, author of *Charlotte
Brontë and the Storyteller's Audience*. As other critics
have noted, Brontë equates characters with their literary experiences; hence, *Jane Eyre* is replete with
their descriptions of books and how characters read
them. Most significantly, by analyzing Jane's literary
endeavors, the reader can chart Jane's development:
As the novel progresses, Jane becomes a more skill-
ful interpreter of text and thus a more successful
teller of tales—in short, a more authoritative narrator of her own life.

As more than one critic has noticed, in *Jane Eyre* the way one
reads is a clue to one's personality. Blanche Ingram appears
fashionably to "beguile, by the spell of fiction, the tedious
hours" of her day but, in fact, does not actually read the book
that she holds before her. In contrast to her social glitter and
personal vacuity, the emotional and mental depth of the
Rivers sisters is signaled by their warm response to Schiller,
while their brother's rigorous self-discipline is suggested by
his daily studies of a Hindustani grammar book. The calm
resignation of Helen Burns is underlined, of course, by her
reading of *Rasselas*, just as Jane's rebellious nature is suggested by her inability to comprehend the same volume.
Eliza Reed studies *The Book of Common Prayer* three times
a day for "the Rubric" only, thus revealing her obsession
with the external forms of conduct and her obliviousness to
the moral roots of behavior in emotion and value. Finally,
and perhaps most obviously, little Jane's vehement description of John Reed as "wicked and cruel . . . like a murderer . . .
like a slave-driver," seems at least partially justified by his si-

Reprinted from *Charlotte Brontë and the Storyteller's Audience*, by Carol Bock, by permission of the University of Iowa Press. Copyright 1992 by University of Iowa Press.

multaneous abuse of both books and people: taking Bewick's *History of British Birds* away from Jane, he first declares exclusive ownership and then violently flings the large volume at her head. *Jane Eyre* thus begins with an impressive demonstration of the power of books and immediately suggests a parallel between one's character and one's literary habits.

The motif also seems to suggest a correlation between one's reading practices and one's proficiency as a storyteller. Like Blanche Ingram, Georgiana Reed uses books to fill up any hiatus in her social existence, but unlike Blanche she is not even capable of keeping up the pretense and falls asleep over her novel. Not surprisingly, Jane contemptuously dismisses Georgiana as a purveyor of self-indulgent pulp fiction and compares her conversation to a "volume of a novel of fashionable life" that "always ran on the same theme—herself, her loves, and woes." Ironically, this theme applies equally well to Jane's own narrative, and the differences between Georgiana and Jane as storytellers may have less to do with their subject matter than with their respective abilities as readers of the world they live in. Jane, we learn from Miss Abbot, "always look[s] as if she were watching everybody, and scheming plots underhand," much like Charlotte's favorite early storyteller, Charles Wellesley/Townshend. Georgiana, on the other hand, is simply too selfish and unimaginative to expend energy on interpreting other people, and her stories about her own experience are consequently shallow and vapid. Mrs. Fairfax, though far from selfish, suffers from a similar lack of interpretive expertise; a poor reader of other people, she is also a poor storyteller who has "no notion of sketching a character."

In contrast, Rochester is apparently able to read much of Jane's nature not only in her face and conduct but in her paintings as well; his wondering questions about her work—"What meaning is that in their solemn depth? . . . Who taught you to paint wind?"—suggest that he is a warmly appreciative interpreter of her character. Clearly a good reader, particularly of Jane, Rochester is also a fluent storyteller. At one point he is shown writing his own life history, which at other times he tells Jane in two sequential narratives, the longest embedded tales in Jane's own story. He also spontaneously concocts the fiction about Jane's supposed new employer, Mrs. Dionysius O'Gall of Bitternutt Lodge, and perplexes Adèle with a highly fanciful account of his relationship with her governess. Perhaps most importantly, in posing as a fortune teller, Rochester becomes reader and storyteller at the same time, just as Jane becomes, simultaneously, both his audience and the text he interprets.

Indeed, next to Jane, Rochester is the most proficient reader-storyteller in the novel, a fact that makes his loss of both hand and sight at the end all the more significant. Unable to write or read, Rochester loses his status as a skilled interpreter at the end of Jane's story when she assumes full responsibility for "gazing for his behalf, and of putting into words . . . the landscape before us." Jane, that is, has complete authority as reader and narrator of the life that she and Rochester share at the end of the novel. His loss of interpretive control over their experience and her concomitant empowerment in this respect mark the triumphant conclusion of Jane's growth toward selfhood, a progress articulated in terms of both sexual politics and literary proficiency. Her story begins when she is literally knocked off her feet by the book that her male cousin throws at her, an efficient way of suggesting Jane's powerlessness as both a female and a reader, and it concludes as she compares herself to Scheherazade, the woman who preserves her own life and liberates her sex through her skill as a teller of tales. A captivating storyteller in the end (perhaps almost literally so), Jane struggles toward literary proficiency from most unpromising beginnings.

GATESHEAD

At Gateshead, reading is a purely consolatory pursuit for young Jane, not simply because it is a refuge from the unhappiness of her actual environment, but also because it allows her to "[draw] parallels," to see analogies in books that help her accept her own experience. Having read Goldsmith's history of Rome, she can compare her cousin to "Nero, Caligula, &c." and describe him in a way that affirms her understanding of his character: "You are like the Roman emperors!" Jane uses books, that is, to confirm her own sense of reality.

But the most puzzling of life's mysteries for Jane is her own self, the alternately searing and chilling moods of passion and despair that characterize her inner experience, and it is especially in an attempt to understand herself that she pursues reading as a little girl. She finds the barren landscapes in Bewick's *British Birds* "profoundly interesting" because they pictorially express her own feelings of isolation and affective deprivation. She is happy in reading Bewick, "happy at least in [her] way," because the book validates her sense of self, morbid and pathetic though it may be. It allows her, in [critic] Norman Holland's terms, to pursue her "identity theme," interpreting books so that they confirm her understanding of experience and thereby strengthen her sense of self-identity. In the descriptive passages in *British Birds*, Jane initially finds an objective correlative for her inner feelings, and reading those passages prepares her to interpret the following illustrations in a satisfying (though, to us, sad) manner: "The words in these introductory pages connected themselves with the succeeding vignettes, and gave significance to the rock standing up alone in a sea of billow and spray; to the broken boat stranded on a desolate coast; to the cold and ghastly moon glancing through bars of cloud at a wreck just sinking." The verbal description of these images of death and isolation prepares Jane to interpret the pictures as personally meaningful to her.

Though Jane can be "happy" in thus confirming her sense of reality through Bewick's, the novel clearly shows that such subjective criticism is dangerous as well as appealing. Jane goes to books, as to life, predisposed to find reflections of her internal reality. The "parallels" she draws are thus often no more than mirror images of her own mind, and reading becomes a solipsistic pursuit in which meaning is imposed rather than discovered or created. This becomes particularly clear in the red room episode, when Jane misinterprets a glimmer of light ("in all likelihood, a gleam from a lantern, carried by some one across the lawn," the older narrator explains) for "a herald of some coming vision from another world." We learn that she has been "prepared . . . for horror," and we suspect not only the ghoulish stories she has heard about "dead men . . . revisiting the earth" but also her recent imaginative wanderings in the "death-white realms" of Bewick's. Predisposed to discover images of death and sterility in her reading, Jane responds subjectively to books and stories, which further disposes her to find such terrifying images in the phenomenal world as well.

Her hysterical breakdown in the red room and the aftermath of that incident reveal precisely how destructive Jane's interpretive habits have become. Once delighted by the world depicted in *Gulliver's Travels*, Jane now sees Gulliver as "a most desolate wanderer in most dread and dangerous regions," that is, as a figure who parallels her own psychic bewilderment. Bessie's songs, also once a source of "lively delight," now convey "an indescribable sadness" because Jane's doleful state of mind accentuates certain refrains "like the saddest cadence of a funeral hymn." Initially attracted to a reading method that seemed to validate her own experience, Jane now discovers that she is incapable of employing any other kind of interpretive strategy, so that all signs yield the same, sad meaning.

After the Bewick/red room episode, Jane is never able to enjoy reading again at Gateshead; in a novel that equates character with the quality of one's literary experience, this surely reflects her dangerously eviscerated sense of self. As compelling and justified as Jane's rebellions at Gateshead appear, they arise, as even little Jane seems to see, not from a sane command of herself in relation to others but from the "madness of [her] conduct, and the dreariness of [her] hated and hating position." Having unleashed her fury at Mrs. Reed after Mr. Brocklehurst's visit, Jane soon regrets her "fierce speaking" and tries to "exercise some better faculty," that is, reading. But she can "make no sense of the subject [of the *Arabian Nights*]; my own thoughts swam always between me and the page," an apt description of a reading experience in which subjectivity is so excessively amplified that it no longer interferes creatively with the text but actually drowns out the storytelling voice. Ironically, the storyteller Jane cannot hear because of her troubled self-absorption is Scheherazade: because she is unable to read in a way that allows her to perceive anything beyond the limited scope of her own experience, Jane cannot recognize, much less imitate, a role model who provides a clear example of how to assert oneself through effective storytelling.

Jane's struggles and quick defeat as a reader at Gateshead are accordingly paralleled by her frustrated attempts as a young storyteller. Prior to her encounter with John Reed over *British Birds*, Jane has apparently been habitually taciturn in her aunt's household. She seems to have been an avid reader of books and a close observer of those around her (much to Abbot's annoyance), but she has "drawn parallels in silence" and "never thought . . . to have declared aloud" her particular reading of people and events at Gateshead. When Jane finally does break silence and offers her cousin a succinct analysis of his character, we may agree with her assessment; but, like Jane, we must concede that her manner of speaking has in fact been counterproductive since it leads directly to her incarceration in the red room. Repeatedly, the young Jane misjudges her task as an explicator of things as she sees them, and though we may admire her honesty and courage, we should perhaps also pity her ineptitude at calculating the effect she will produce when she addresses her listeners.

Jane understandably wishes to create a compelling narrative about Mrs. Reed's cruel treatment of her (as ultimately she does, of course, in writing her autobiography); but instead of persuasively telling her tale to a potentially sympathetic audience like Mr. Lloyd, she unwisely announces her intention to the very person she hopes to discredit: "I shall remember how you . . . thrust me back into the red-room, and locked me up there. . . . *I will tell* anybody who asks me questions *this exact tale*" (emphasis added). When the apothecary does ask questions about her life at Gateshead, however, she discovers that she can neither examine her experience critically nor articulate it in a rational yet expressive manner. She therefore stumbles through an account of her feelings that is sadly deficient when contrasted against the powerful story the adult narrator has told, and the productive result of her conversation with Mr. Lloyd—Jane's being sent away to school—is largely attributable to his skill as an auditor rather than to her proficiency as a speaker. The fact that, despite Jane's bumbling speech, her interchange with the apothecary produces truth suggests how imperative it is that an audience be responsive to the teller's tale, that readers be actively engaged in interpreting the text before them. Mr. Lloyd does not simply affirm Jane's story—indeed, he repeatedly opposes her interpretation of events and accuses her of being "a baby" and "silly"; but he does engage her in a vigorous discussion of the reality she must face and thus helps Jane create a verbal arena in which truth can emerge and solutions to her predicament be considered.

But Jane rarely enjoys the luxury of such a skilled and disinterested audience. Mrs. Reed repeatedly orders her to be quiet, and others often either speak for her—as Bessie does when she answers the first questions Mr. Lloyd puts to Jane—or tell her how to speak—as when John instructs her to "Say, 'What do you want, Master Reed?'" And while Mr. Brocklehurst does not apply the brutal methods of silencing and censoring Jane's speech that the Gateshead inhabitants do, his interlocutory style is one that just as effectively transforms the potential storyteller into a mute and helpless object of his own interpretive maneuvers.

While ostensibly trying to draw Jane out, Mr. Brocklehurst asks questions that neatly play into the Gateshead reading of her character and make it difficult for the child to assert her own interpretation of herself. Asked if she is a good girl, Jane finds it "impossible to reply to this in the affirmative" since her "little world held a contrary opinion." Her silence allows Mrs. Reed to supply a negative response to this first, crucial question in their conversation. Predisposed to see people—especially children placed under his authority—as fallen creatures, Mr. Brocklehurst finds gratifying confirmation of his views in Mrs. Reed's assessment and proceeds to investigate Jane's character according to the assumption that she is, in fact, "a naughty child." When questioned about her reading habits, Jane responds promptly and decisively only to be told that her literary tastes are "shocking" proof of her wickedness. Clearly, the intent of this conversation is to confirm Mr. Brocklehurst's narrow, preformed interpretation of Jane's character rather than to give her the opportunity to express herself.

As Jane is preparing to respond to his recommendation that she exchange her wicked heart for a good one, Mrs. Reed characteristically preempts the child's part in the discussion, which, nevertheless, continues to focus on Jane's unsatisfactory "character and disposition." The combined forces of Mr. Brocklehurst's coercive questioning and Aunt Reed's interdiction completely silence Jane, preventing her from even trying to tell her own story. Instead, she becomes the subject of the interpretive biases of her two unfavorably disposed critics. Looking on helplessly, Jane knows that she can do "nothing, indeed," to correct their misreadings of her character since she has been deprived of all interpretive authority in this storytelling situation. As she recognizes, Mrs. Reed and Mr. Brocklehurst have "transformed" her not only into a maliciously misinterpreted story—a victimized text, if you will—but also into a mute, secondary audience to a libelous account of herself. Appropriating Jane's rightful role as storyteller of her own experience, Mrs. Reed tells her primary audience, Mr. Brocklehurst, that the child is a liar and explains to Jane that "I mention this in your hearing . . . that you may not attempt to impose on Mr. Brocklehurst." Since Aunt Reed and Mr. Brocklehurst have imposed their view of reality on Jane rather than the other way around, this latter statement is, of course, bitingly ironic. In the triadic configuration of teller-text-audience that makes up the literary experience, this scene portrays Jane both as an abused text subject to the hermeneutic [interpretative] impositions of hostile readers and as a disempowered audience incapable of correcting the false narrative that two ill-motivated storytellers tell each other in her presence.

In contrast to Mr. Lloyd's conversation with Jane, the verbal arena that Mr. Brocklehurst and Mrs. Reed create is one that sacrifices truth to power. Jane's description of the retaliation following Mr. Brocklehurst's visit underscores the political nature of their discussion about Jane: having forced Mrs. Reed from the breakfast room by an explosion of "fierce speaking," Jane is left "winner of the field," free to muse in "conqueror's solitude" on the "battle . . . fought" and the "victory . . . gained." A characteristically chilling reaction of remorse soon follows the pleasures of vengeance, however, and the delicious sensation of speaking hateful words is replaced by the "metallic and corroding" aftertaste of poisoned speech. Having driven the enemy from the field, the storyteller regretfully finds that she has no audience with whom to interact; she must learn to tell her view of the truth in a manner that will captivate rather than assault.

Not coincidently, just when Jane realizes how dramatically she has failed in this way, she also discovers that she is no longer capable of reading. Sadly putting down the *Arabian Nights*, she walks out of the house and attempts to read the face of nature instead. But there in the frozen landscape she encounters the same images, symbolically reflecting the same theme that has persistently interfered with her appreciation of other symbolic texts: "I found no pleasure in the silent trees, the fallen fir-cones, the congealed relics of autumn, russet leaves, swept by past winds in heaps, and now stiffened together. I leaned against a gate, and looked into an empty field where no sheep were feeding, where the short grass was nipped and blanched. . . . I stood, a wretched child enough, whispering to myself over and over again, 'What shall I do?—what shall I do?'"

READING AT LOWOOD

The answer to that question is revealed, of course, in the next section of Jane's narrative, which tells of her experience at Lowood. There she begins to learn a new way of reading, one that will assist in the reformation of her identity theme and prepare her to become a more authoritative narrator of her own life. In contrast to the private and consolatory nature of Jane's reading at Gateshead, reading at Lowood is a communal activity in which everyone is expected to participate. Jane's first view of her schoolmates is that of eighty female readers uniformly dressed and simultaneously engaged in conning their lesson books. The next morning, she sees them "all drawn up in four semicircles . . . all [holding] books in their hands" and waiting for the school bell to ring so they may start the "business" of reading together, a scene that suggests a radically different reading environment for the child accustomed to smuggling books into a "hiding-place" like the window seat at Gateshead.

Reading at Lowood usually entails a collective effort in which the group as a whole or a recognized authority such as a teacher or senior student reads an authoritative text or recites it out loud. The act of reading aloud in the presence of others transforms each reader into a kind of storyteller whose audience is, like herself, both reading and narrating at the same time. The situation has parallels, of course, in Brontë's own school experience as well as in the storytelling situation she shared with Branwell, Emily, and Anne. Charlotte's siblings were a creatively refractory audience, however, whose noisy interpretive responses ensured the protean growth of their tales. At Lowood, a deadening concern with factual trivia and matters of form silence such interpretive noise, as Helen Burns discovers when she is asked "questions about tonnage and poundage, and ship-money" and sent to the bottom of the class for "some error of pronunciation or some inattention to stops."

Indeed, while each reader must become engaged in the transmission of texts to her audience of fellow readers and thereby adopts an active role like that of a storyteller, in fact, the simultaneous reading and narrating of works at Lowood comprise an essentially passive act designed to confirm the values of the community through mechanical repetition of canonical texts. Immediately upon rising each morning the girls "[form] in a file, two and two" to hear prayers read aloud and then are ordered to "form classes!" for more exercise in reading. Appropriately, lessons begin each day with the repetition of the Collect, a brief prayer whose original purpose was to facilitate the gathering of worshippers so that they might proceed to church en masse. After this, "certain texts of scripture were *said*, and to these succeeded a protracted reading of . . . the Bible" (emphasis added). The emphasis on the repetition, recitation, and "saying" of authoritative texts suggests that reading is not a creative, interpretive pursuit at Lowood but one that relies on memorization and rote practice to maintain an orderly, conventional consensus about the nature of reality.

Despite the negative features of the reading methods prescribed at Lowood, they appear to have some salutary effect on Jane, for they serve as a check against her previous, dangerous interpretive habits. An insistence upon group work discourages the morbidly introspective reading Jane has grown familiar with and forces her to participate in a communal literary experience. Reading at Lowood is thus a social act that helps define Jane's relationship to others rather than a solipsistic experience that destructively confirms her separateness. But like her life in general at Lowood, this new way of reading is only a partial help to Jane, and her need to be creatively engaged in the literary endeavor must also be fulfilled.

HELEN BURNS

Because of this need, Jane is immediately attracted to Helen Burns, who, like herself at Gateshead, reads in quiet isolation from the rest of the group. "Her occupation," Jane remarks, "touched a chord of sympathy somewhere; for I too liked reading." Indeed, the first event of their relationship is an act of joint textual interpretation. In contrast to John Reed, who grabs a book away from Jane and then hits her with it, Helen gently hands her friend the volume of *Rasselas* she has shown interest in with no more interpretive commentary than the unassuming remark, "I like it." When Jane demonstrates an apparent lack of appreciation for the text, Helen merely takes it back "quietly, and without saying anything" resumes reading. Here, a text is a means for bringing together two readers in a situation that allows for diversity of response. Each girl apparently holds to her own reading of the work, but neither claims authority over the text as John

Reed does in declaring exclusive ownership; nor does one reader attempt to impose her interpretation upon the other as John Reed also dramatically does when he hurls the book at his cousin's head.

Though their interchange about *Rasselas* appears egalitarian, Helen is really something more than Jane's peer in reading, however. Being older, she has more literary experience and consequently greater skill as an interpreter of texts, a fact the younger child implicitly acknowledges through her eager questions about the inscription over the Lowood door. Helen demonstrates her proficiency as a reader most convincingly when she analyzes Jane herself. She rejects Brocklehurst's characterization of her friend as a liar, "for I read a sincere nature in your ardent eyes and . . . clear front," and also sees that Jane is "too impulsive, too vehement," and too needy of the "love of [other] human beings." Having listened to Jane's account of Mrs. Reed, Helen wisely explains that "she has been unkind to you . . . because . . . she dislikes your cast of character," an analysis that the mature narrator has already presented: "I thus suffered [because] . . . I was a discord in Gateshead-hall: I was like nobody there. . . . They were not bound to regard with affection a thing . . . opposed to them in temperament, in capacity, in propensities."

Helen also notes that Jane is "but a little untaught girl" who will probably change her mind as she grows older, a comment less remarkable for its perceptiveness than for its power to confirm Helen's authority in judging Jane. Growth from immaturity and ignorance to a changed, mature perspective is precisely what readers of the genre to which *Jane Eyre* belongs expect, and, besides, such growth has already been signaled by the knowing interventions of the older narrator. Helen's skill as an interpreter of Jane's personality is thus validated both by the generic conventions that readers expect to find in the text and by a narrative perspective that reinforces those expectations.

Given the correlation between reading and storytelling in *Jane Eyre*, it is almost predictable that Helen should also turn out to be Jane's first guide in the art of telling tales. Emboldened by Helen's kindness, Jane recounts her experience at Gateshead with characteristic vehemence: "I proceeded . . . to pour out in my own way, the tale of my sufferings and resentments . . . [speaking] as I felt, without reserve or softening." Unable to respond favorably to Jane's "bitter and truculent" manner of telling her tale, Helen at first makes no reply, just as she had made no comment on Jane's apparent lack of appreciation for *Rasselas*. When confronted with Jane's impatient demand for audience response, however, she remarks that, from her perspective, certain parts of the narrative seem excessive. Warned by Helen's response, Jane is later able to revise her narrative so that it seems more credible and hence produces the desired effect on Miss Temple:

> I resolved in the depth of my heart that I would be most moderate: most correct; and, having reflected a few minutes in order to arrange coherently what I had to say, I told her all the story of my sad childhood. . . . My language was more subdued than it generally was when it developed that sad theme; and mindful of Helen's warnings . . . , I infused into the narrative far less of gall and wormwood than ordinary. Thus restrained and simplified, it sounded more credible: I felt as I went on that Miss Temple fully believed me.

For the first time, Jane has not been blindly preoccupied with her need to validate herself and her experience but has considered the perceptions of those whom she has invited to participate in the unfolding of her story. She has learned to anticipate audience response somewhat and to "arrange" her narrative so that the truth as she sees it will also be apparent to her listener.

SUCCESSFUL STORYTELLING

Jane is immediately rewarded for her first success at storytelling by being given those things she most desperately needs: a reassuring kiss from a loving, respected mother figure; nourishing and delicious food to eat; and a place by a warm fireside. But even more important to Jane's development is her presence during the following "conversation . . . between [Miss Temple] and Helen, which it was indeed a privilege to be admitted to hear." Once again, Jane is cast in the role of silent, secondary audience, but this time the subject of discussion is not herself but "books: how many they had read!"—and not only those of English authors, but also French and, to Jane's unbound astonishment, Latin writers as well. Having followed Helen and the appropriately named Miss Temple through dark and "intricate passages," Jane has entered the sanctum of the head teacher's private apartment, has passed the first test of telling her tale, has "feasted . . . on nectar and ambrosia," and now becomes initiated into the full mystery of the arts she is apparently appointed to perform. Listening to Helen translate Virgil, Jane's amazement turns to "veneration" as she hears a reader creatively transform an ostensibly indecipherable text into an articulate, meaningful tale.

Jane's silent participation in the conversation between Helen Burns and Miss Temple thus allows her to see the literary experience in a new way. In contrast to her Gateshead habits, books here bring people together, and interpretation becomes a creative act performed for the mutual delight of all participants. That these activities are conducted by a highly exclusive group in a private, almost sacred place suggests that those involved are, indeed, privileged individuals with unusual powers, reminiscent perhaps of the little Brontë children themselves. This quality, in addition to the pleasurable intimacy of the environment—the nourishing presence of food, warmth, and physical affection—sharply contrasts with the reading and storytelling methods practiced in the Lowood classroom. Neither dangerously solipsistic nor oppressive due to an insistence on conformity, the acts of reading and storytelling Jane witnesses in Miss Temple's room counter the extremist paradigms represented at Gateshead and Lowood respectively and provide a model for Jane's newly aroused aspirations.

The episode in Miss Temple's apartment thus marks an important turn in Jane's development and underscores the centrality of storytelling and reading to the heroine's struggle for self-actualization. Appropriately, one of her first scholastic efforts at Lowood is to learn how to translate French, an activity that fuses the interpretive skills of reading with the expressive craft of storytelling. No longer hampered by a purely solipsistic method of interpretation or silenced by an ineffectual rhetorical stance, Jane simultaneously becomes a successful reader and storyteller when she learns to translate "the first two tenses of the verb *Etre.*" She learns to interpret and articulate the meaning of the phrases "I am" and "I was"—that is, to understand and tell the story of what she is and has been—rather than remain the object of other people's interpretations. Interpretive and expressive talents thus emerge as the essential elements of Jane's character, the core of her self, which she must preserve at all costs. Her further experiences, first at Thornfield and then at Marsh End, demonstrate how difficult such self-preservation can be.

CHAPTER 3

Important Themes in *Jane Eyre*

READINGS ON
JANE EYRE

Christian Themes in *Jane Eyre*

Norman Sherry

Many critics have noted that *Jane Eyre* exhibits features of Romanticism and the Gothic novel, two literary movements of the nineteenth century. Yet amid these stylistic trappings, notes critic Norman Sherry, Charlotte Brontë explores serious questions about morality, spirituality, and individual choice. For example, when tempted to remain in an adulterous relationship with Rochester, Jane states, "I will keep the law given by God. . . . Laws and principles are not for times when there is no temptation." Driven by her Christian principles, then, Jane flees Thornfield to avoid an unholy union with the man she loves—despite agonizingly painful consequences. Jane's words and courageous actions, Sherry writes, prove her resolute determination to obey the tenets of God and religion.

The source material that went into the making of [*Jane Eyre*] is very mixed. From Charlotte's own experience, there is obviously the period at the Clergy Daughters' School, and the life at Haworth Parsonage, as well as her teaching days. But much of what makes up the novel is conventional in the fictional sense. There are well-established literary sources which demand a specific and strong response from the reader.

Jane is a Cinderella figure to begin with, without the beauty of a Cinderella, but with all the sympathy such a figure draws through being pushed aside, ill-treated and ignored. And her story, with its gradual recognition of her virtues and strengths, is the romantic tale of Cinderella who marries her prince. But it is also, in part, the story of Pamela (of whom Jane is told by Bessie), the servant girl of Richardson's novel who resists her master's attempts to seduce her

Excerpted from chapter 4, "*Jane Eyre*," of *Charlotte and Emily Brontë*, by Norman Sherry (London: Evans Brothers). Copyright © 1969 by Norman Sherry. Reprinted by permission of the author.

and eventually becomes his wife. This basis in romantic folk-tale and the novel of seduction gives the story a great deal of its fascination.

On one level we have all the trappings—in the central section especially—of the Gothic horror novel. There is the 'demoniac laugh—low, suppressed, and deep-uttered, as it seemed, at the very keyhole of [her] chamber door'; the mysterious apartment on the third floor; Mason with one arm 'almost soaked in blood', with a 'corpse-like face'; the mad woman who 'grovelled, seemingly, on all fours'.

In this situation Jane Eyre is as cool and courageous as any Gothic heroine. She puts out the fire in Rochester's bed, and sits alone with Mason in the night bathing his wounded arm.

In Rochester, there is something of Richardson's rakes—Mr. B. and Lovelace, and of the Gothic villain. But there is also something of the Byronic hero with his rough charm, mysterious background, his wild life, brusque, often cruel manner, but tragic and strong emotions.

All of these are, individually, good 'story-lines'. Brought together they make a powerful mixture. And there is no sense of their clashing since all draw upon the same fundamental emotional response and are united in the strong, passionate figure of Jane.

But this same novel, made up of such popular and traditional literary elements, was to call forth from some reviewers such accusations as: 'Pre-eminently an anti-Christian composition' . . . a murmering against . . . God's appointment' and 'an undue reliance on self, unamiable . . . if not positively irreligious.' This draws our attention to other, more serious tones in the novel, to concerns with more fundamental issues than those of the pathetic or Gothic tale.

THE QUESTION POSED

Serious questions about life and morals are constantly being posed in the midst of the romantic and Gothic situations. How is one to live within the situation in which God has placed one? How does one suffer tyranny, cruelty? How does one control strong emotion? How does one live in barren circumstances? How does one keep one's religious and moral integrity, while still satisfying the individual sense of justice and rightness? Does one rebel, as the young Jane does? accept with Christian meekness as Helen does? become a liar and hypocrite for the sake of a piece of gingerbread? control one's passions to obey God's precepts no matter what the personal cost?

This serious vein of philosophical inquiry about life is an important part of the novel. It is revealed for example in the pronouncements about the guiding principles of religion and morals which arise from a conversation or as a result of an incident. Thus Mr. Rochester, speaking of his determination to change his aim and motives in life, states that he will pass a law that both these are right:

'They cannot be, sir, if they require a new statute to legalise them.' [says Jane]

'They are, Miss Eyre, though they absolutely require a new statute: unheard-of combinations of circumstances demand unheard-of rules.'

'That sounds a dangerous maxim, sir; because one can see at once that it is liable to abuse . . .' You are human and fallible . . . The human and fallible should not arrogate a power with which the divine and perfect alone can be safely entrusted.'

'What power?'

'That of saying of any strange, unsanctioned line of action, "Let it be right."'

Such inquiry and such attempts to answer fundamental questions take place on the childish level with the young Jane:

'Do you know where the wicked go after death?'

'They go to hell,' was my ready and orthodox answer.

'And what is hell? Can you tell me that?'

'A pit full of fire.'

'And should you like to fall into that pit, and to be burning there for ever?'

'No, sir.'

'What must you do to avoid it?'

I deliberated a moment: my answer, when it did come was objectionable: 'I must keep in good health, and not die.'

Again, a conversation with St. John involves a discussion of the types of philosopher:

'You would describe yourself as a mere pagan philosopher,' I said.

'No. There is this difference between me and deistic philosophers: I believe; and I believe the Gospel. You missed your epithet. I am not a pagan, but a Christian philosopher—a follower of the sect of Jesus. As His disciple I adopt His pure, His merciful, His benignant doctrines . . .'

Far from being an anti-Christian novel, therefore, *Jane*

Eyre is concerned throughout with questions of moral and Christian behaviour, to an even greater extent than was *The Professor*. And while, in the first novel, God was a distant observer of his creatures, He becomes here an active participant in the action. The characters are much aware of God and His teachings, and interpret His will and doctrines in terms of their own fate and actions.

So we have Bessie's song of the orphan child, early in the novel, pointing to Jane's orphaned and lonely path in life:

> Ev'n should I fall o'er the broken bridge passing,
> Or stray in the marshes, by false lights beguiled,
> Still will my Father, with promise and blessing,
> Take to his bosom the poor orphan child.

And so Jane, having left Rochester, concludes: 'God must have led me on', and 'Sure was I of His efficiency to save what He had made.' And so St. John mistakenly concludes: 'God and nature intended you for a missionary's wife.' And so Rochester tells her, eventually, 'Of late, Jane—only—only of late—I began to see and acknowledge the hand of God in my doom.'

There is, also, a strong sense of God's justice at work *in this life* in terms of punishment and reward, rather than in an afterlife. Though Helen Burns looks to happiness in a future life, Rochester's maiming and blinding, Jane's wanderings and sufferings, and their ultimate reunion take place in this world.

Thus God, often working through accident or nature, is very much present in the world of the novel.

PATH OF THE HEROINE THROUGH LIFE

Jane Eyre's story, as well as being that of a romantic and Gothic heroine is also a progression in moral and spiritual terms. The situations in which she finds herself require that she should learn a Christian attitude to her own nature and to life, and she is tested in this learning. Her marriage to Rochester not merely the conventionally romantic union of the novel, but a coming together of two sinners who have repented and suffered and whose union is thus sanctioned by God.

Choice in this novel is no longer a matter of leaving a job on moral grounds, but of obeying the precepts of God and religion—and of one's own nature—in the face of the direct consequences. Nor does Jane find a Christian attitude to life easy, as Crimsworth did. 'False lights' do beguile, and thus the smugness of the earlier novel is avoided.

The first part of *Jane Eyre* can be seen in terms of a learning process, the second in terms of putting the knowledge gained into practice.

Jane Eyre has certain strong characteristics. She is passionate and imaginative—human sympathies and affections have a powerful hold on her. She thinks 'too much of the love of human beings'. She longs for a wide experience of life. She is clear-sighted and candid; she cannot dissemble or be deceitful.

She begins with these natural propensities, but at first, being in a false situation and without knowledge or learning, she is wild and unhappy. She has pagan ideas of reacting to hurts—an eye for an eye and a tooth for a tooth: 'I will never call you aunt again as long as I live. I will never come to see you when I am grown up; and if any one asks me how I liked you, and how you treated me, I will say the very thought of you makes me sick, and that you treated me with miserable cruelty,' she tells Mrs. Reed. So she successfully routs her aunt, but she realises that such a doctrine of revenge does not make for happiness. Mrs. Reed leaves her in possession of the field, but unrestrained passion leads inevitably to the reaction: 'A child cannot quarrel with its elders . . . cannot give its furious feelings uncontrolled play . . . without experiencing afterwards the pang of remorse and the chill of reaction.' As a result of the treatment she receives and her reaction to it, she feels only bad emotions surging in her breast.

At Lowood, Helen Burns undergoes a greater cruelty and tyranny, but she tells Jane: 'It is not violence that best overcomes hate—nor vengeance that most certainly heals injury . . . Love your enemies; bless them that curse you; do good to them that hate you and despitefully use you.'

From Helen, Jane learns to bear shame without showing her suffering, she learns to control her hatred when telling Miss Temple her story, but she cannot share Helen's rejection of the world, or her logical view of a matter. When Helen points out that not everybody believes Jane a liar since only eighty have heard her called so, Jane objects, 'But what have I to do with millions! The eighty I know despise me.' And she goes on, '. . . if others don't love me, I would rather die than live.'

It is from Miss Temple that Jane learns how to control her passionate nature: 'I had imbibed from her something of her nature and much of her habits; more harmonious thoughts;

what seemed better regulated feelings . . . I appeared a disciplined and subdued character.'

Thus, when she leaves Lowood, she has learned to control her nature while retaining those aspects of it which are good; she has still the 'power to be tranquil' when there is a 'reason for tranquillity'. But her learning has not been tested. It is tested at Thornfield. On the grounds of her learning in moral and religious principle, Jane gives Rochester excellent theoretical advice: '. . . nothing free-born would submit to [insolence], even for a salary'; 'Repentance is said to be [remorse's] cure'.

In reply, Rochester calls her a 'neophyte, that have not passed the porch of life, and are absolutely unacquainted with its mysteries.'

IDOLATRY AND THE LAW GIVEN BY GOD

The world for her is to be Thornfield Hall, and her testing is to be in terms of that craving for love which she has always felt. She shows herself equal to the occasion. She can control her emotions even under Mr. Rochester's pretence of being in love with Blanche Ingram, but once his love for her is declared, she gives hers whole-heartedly: 'My future husband was becoming my whole world . . . almost my hope of heaven. He stood between me and every thought of religion, as an eclipse intervenes between man and the broad sun. I could not, in those days, see God for His Creature: of whom I had made an idol.' She is falling into the sin of idolatry— the failing of her passionate nature.

After the broken marriage ceremony comes Jane's greatest testing. Is idolatry to win? If she leaves him, she is faced with immense suffering: a suffering increased by the knowledge of *his* suffering and the further degradation he might be led to. All that is required of her, to obtain their mutual happiness, is the transgression of 'a mere human law'. And Jane reflects, 'Who in the world cares for *you*? or who will be injured by what you do?' It is a mere matter of a convention to be broken.

But her answer takes her back to that principle she earlier enunciated to Rochester: 'The human and fallible should not arrogate a power with which the divine and perfect alone can be safely entrusted . . . That of saying of any strange, unsanctioned line of action "Let it be right." '

And she answers:

> '*I* care for myself. The more solitary . . . the more I will respect
> myself. I will keep the law given by God; sanctioned by man
> . . . Laws and principles are not for times when there is no
> temptation: they are for such moments as this, when body
> and soul rise in mutiny against their rigour . . .

The action she takes—right though it may be to her—is most
difficult in that she 'had no solace from self-approbation;
none even from self-respect'.

Religion Calls

With the Rivers family, Jane achieves something of the equilibrium of her years with Miss Temple. She has now a 'small
independence', she has a home, and she has affection from
the Rivers sisters. Passion is controlled. Life is to be a shel-
tered and moderate existence. But a further testing is due—
this time in the other direction. Passion must be given up altogether, independence, life itself, in the dedication of her
life to God's work as a missionary.

In trying to persuade her to this loveless existence, St.
John is as mistaken to her nature as was Rochester, who
tried to dress her in jewels and silks and put her in the position of his former mistresses: 'God and nature [says St. John)
intended you for a missionary's wife. It is not personal, but
mental endowments they have given you: you are formed for
labour, not for love.' For both Rochester and St John, she is
to be the 'instrument' of good: 'But the instrument—the instrument! God, who does the work, ordains the instrument.
I have myself—I tell it you without parable—been a worldly,
dissipated, restless man; and I believe I have found the instrument for my cure' [says Rochester]. And Jane objects to
St. John's plan on the grounds that: 'He prizes me as a soldier would a good weapon, and that is all . . . such a martyrdom would be monstrous.'

Yet, under the pressures St. John puts upon her, she almost yields: 'I was tempted to cease struggling with him—to
rush down the torrent of his will into the gulf of his existence, and there lose my own. I was almost as hard beset by
him now as I had been once before, in a different way, by another [Rochester]. I was a fool both times. To have yielded
then would have been an error of principle; to have yielded
now would have been an error of judgment.' But 'Religion
called—Angels beckoned—God commanded—life rolled together like a scroll—death's gates opening showed eternity

beyond . . .' It is the vision and sacrifice of Helen Burns.

But the voice of Rochester calling to her, breaks the spell: 'Down superstition . . . This is not thy deception, nor thy witch-craft: it is the work of nature. She was roused, and did—no miracle—but her best.'

Rochester, maimed and blinded, but now acknowledging God's goodness, is a fit mate for Jane, who has also gone through the tempering fire of misery and temptation.

A PILGRIM'S PROGRESS

Thus the pathetic and Gothic story is the vehicle for demonstrating the working out of a Christian theme. Viewed in this way, *Jane Eyre* is an unusual novel, since it is a kind of pilgrim's progress presented in terms of the Gothic and romantic world and of passionate sexual love. It is an allegory in the sense that it is a moral and religious discourse under the guise of a popular novel.

But it is not a progress towards spirituality and the renunciation of this world. The two major temptations undergone by Jane are first towards the passionate and worldly in defiance of God's laws, and secondly towards the dedicated and spiritual in defiance of her own nature. Jane can accept neither. The allegory is a defence of the individual's right to seek his own way—worldly or other-worldly—provided he transgresses no divine law in doing this.

In her preface to the second edition, Charlotte Brontë made clear this concern of hers with a moral theme. She attacks those who have criticised the novel, those 'whose ears detect in each protest against bigotry—that parent of crime— an insult to piety, that regent of God on earth'. She then states 'certain simple truths':

> Conventionality is not morality, self-righteousness is not religion. To attack the first is not to assail the last. To pluck the mask from the face of the Pharisee, is not to lift an impious hand to the Crown of Thorns . . . appearance should not be mistaken for truth; narrow human doctrines . . . should not be substituted for the world-redeeming creed of Christ.

Whatever intentions she may have had in writing the novel to create something 'wild, wonderful, and thrilling', this firmly moral and religious view could not be kept out.

Death and Survival in *Jane Eyre*

Robert Keefe

Jane Eyre exhibits a strong fixation on death, suggests Robert Keefe, author of *Charlotte Brontë's World of Death*, in which the following critical analysis appears. This fixation, Keefe writes, perhaps mirrors Brontë's own attitude toward death and separation. Like her orphaned heroine Jane, Brontë's own loss of family, including a beloved sister and mother, was a powerful influence in her life. *Jane Eyre*, then, serves as a vehicle through which Brontë explores her ambivalent, complex feelings about death, survivor's guilt, and an individual's efforts to resist the will to die.

For more than a hundred years, critics have recognized that one portion of *Jane Eyre* is particularly relevant to the author's life. Lowood is an imaginative rendering of Cowan Bridge, the school where Charlotte's two older sisters died. Charlotte herself admitted as much, telling Elizabeth Gaskell, moreover, that Helen Burns, Jane's Lowood companion, was an "exact transcript" of her sister Maria. We have seen the complex nature of Charlotte's reaction to the death of her beloved sister. That reaction, it seems to me, provides the creative impulse behind *Jane Eyre*.

Lowood is Jane's Valley of the Shadow of Death, a charnel house where typhus strikes down forty-five out of eighty girls. But Jane wanders through it unscathed. She will later be reproached for her survival. Sarah Reed will complain: "What did they do with [Jane] at Lowood? The fever broke out there, and many of the pupils died. She, however, did not die; but I . . . wish she had died!" The accusation is, in all probability, an echo of an indictment which a corner of

Charlotte Brontë's mind had been making for two decades. For Charlotte, like Jane, refused to die with the others, held on to life with a tenacity which at times must have seemed criminal to her. Sarah Reed gives voice to the accusation which lies at the heart of *Jane Eyre*, the complex problem of survival with which Brontë attempts to come to terms in the novel.

Helen Burns is of course the most important one of those who die at Lowood. Most critics have accepted Charlotte's idealized portrait of her sister at face value, seeing Helen's influence as beneficial to Jane's development. The issue is more complicated than that, however; certainly the little girl is a saint, but that very sainthood is an insidious threat to Jane. For Helen Burns is a creature in love with death. The little admirer of Dr. Johnson's pessimistic tome, *Rasselas*, tries to demonstrate to her friend that all of life is vanity, that no satisfaction is to be found on this earth. Only death will bring fulfillment: "Debasement and sin will fall from us with this cumbrous frame of flesh, and only the spark of spirit will remain. [My creed] makes Eternity a rest—a mighty home, not a terror and an abyss." It is an ingenious solution to the problems of life. The believer can find a parent in God, a rest and a home in Heaven. And all one need do to attain these rewards is die. Despite her benevolence, Jane's friend is a Christian siren who would lure the young pilgrim to her death on the rocks of sanctity.

But Brontë's protagonist is tough-minded. On the day before Helen's death, Jane returns to the school after a romp in the woods. The very fact that so many are dying around them has made life easier for the survivors: "We did what we liked, went where we liked: we lived better too." Some die and some live, and the removal of the dead gives the survivors a spacious freedom they had not known before. It apparently gives them guilt, too, but Jane does not know that. She does realize, however, that life is preferable to death. The sight of the surgeon's pony at the door of Lowood sets off a meditation on which is central to the meaning of the novel: "How sad to be lying now on a sick bed, and to be in danger of dying! This world is pleasant—it would be dreary to be called from it, and to have to go who knows where?" Helen knows where and is willing to die. But she would rather not die alone. That same evening, just before midnight, Jane goes to her friend's sickroom. The scene contains echoes of the Angrian fixation on corpses: "I advanced; then paused by the crib side: my hand was on the curtain, but I preferred speaking before I withdrew it. I still recoiled at the dread of seeing a corpse."

Helen is still alive, though barely. To Jane's naïve question— "Are you going somewhere, Helen? Are you going home?"— she gives an alluring answer: "Yes; to my long home—my last home. . . . God is my father . . . You will come to the same region of happiness: be received by the same mighty, universal Parent, no doubt, dear Jane. . . . Don't leave me, Jane: I like to have you near me." Jane makes a promise she cannot, in the nature of things, keep: "I'll stay with you, *dear* Helen: no one shall take me away." But her love is not strong enough; she falls asleep and the nurse carries the child away from the now stiffening corpse. The living cannot remain truly faithful to the dead. Years later Jane will provide Helen's grave with a stone on which is written *Resurgam*—"I shall arise." Jane will remember Helen and regret her death. But she will not join her in any shadowy afterlife if she can help it.

The ambivalence of Charlotte's attitude toward her saintly sister Maria shows through the idealization of the portrait. And near the center of that ambivalence there seems to be a feeling that Maria provided her with an example which she could not, would not follow.

The demise of Helen Burns is of course not in itself the cause of Jane's terror of death. Something has happened years before that event to sharpen her natural instinct to remain alive. Jane has seen death before, and it fascinates and repels her. In the years prior to the opening of the novel, her parents had died. As narrator, Jane lingers over Helen's death, but passes quickly, almost cursorily, over that earlier loss. Her narrative strategy thus resembles Brontë's own attitude toward the death of her mother and her oldest sister: the loss of a sibling provides reinforcement and focus for feelings which originate as repressed reactions to an earlier death, one which is too painful to dwell on.

We can only conjecture, however, about the actual origins of Jane's guilt feelings: perhaps like her creator's, they derive from parental loss. But their origin is unimportant. The crucial point is that Brontë's most famous heroine serves as a vehicle for working off her own guilt feelings, her own complex attraction for and horror of death. And we have seen where these feelings come from.

As opposed to her rather pedestrian forerunner, William Crimsworth, Jane Eyre inhabits an immense mental universe. She sees her life in apocalyptic terms, hovering precariously in this Middle Kingdom of Earth, avoiding both Hell and Heaven. In her world defeat would not be, as in *The Professor*, temporary bankruptcy; it would be eternal damnation. But victory, too, poses a threat to Jane's integrity, a threat which has been largely overlooked in criticism of the novel. Her avoidance of Helen's example is part of a larger pattern in the novel. Death holds a strong attraction for Jane, and it is this inner compulsion to die which she fights off throughout the novel, not simply external threats. Her need for exoneration from some shadowy guilt opens her up to the temptation of becoming a Christian martyr and submitting to a righteous death in order to be taken off to Heaven.

MORAL STRUGGLE

The catechism scene with Brocklehurst provides a good example of Jane's dilemma:

"What must you do to avoid [Hell]?"

"I must keep in good health and not die."

Jane's answer is a childish expression of a complex problem. In order to prove her innocence, Jane has to confront her sense of sin. At the same time, in order to live, she has to conquer her own need to die. Thus in Jane's mind, the will to avoid death and the will to believe in her innocence coalesce. To grow sick and die would simply be the logical consequence of her sense of guilt; to remain healthy is a moral struggle in the face of her need to punish herself for crimes whose nature she does not understand. Therefore she cannot give Brocklehurst the answer he wants; she cannot tell him that she will be good and go to Heaven. For Heaven, like Hell, presupposes death.

Much of what earlier criticism thought of as Jane's dreamy, romantic nature can be traced back to this fixation on death. It shows up in the books she chooses to read, the poems she remembers, the artifacts she looks at, the art she herself creates. The paintings she shows to Rochester provide a good example of the texture of her mind.

But not just *Jane*'s mind. In a seminal article on the paintings, Laurence E. Moser suggests that the pictures can be fruitfully examined with the aid of "the surrealistic tenet that art of necessity mirrors the artist's personality and mentality, in this case both Jane's and Charlotte's, and tends violently toward a complete revelation of self." Moser's point is well taken. And, as he notes, what the paintings reveal about Jane and Charlotte is their attitude toward death and separation.

THE PAINTINGS

The second painting seems the most mysterious. Unlike the first and the third there seems to be no drive toward narrative in the second picture at all. It is, Jane tells us, a symbolic portrait of the evening star: "Rising into the sky was a woman's shape to the bust. . . . The dim forehead was crowned with a star; . . . the eyes shone dark and wild; the hair streamed shadowy, like a beamless cloud torn by storm or by electric travail." The seemingly threatening supernatural figure will appear in other guises throughout the novel—as the moon, as Mother Nature, as an anthropomorphic figure whom Jane calls "Mother." Throughout the novel the sky will be filled with cosmic reactions to, and portents of, Jane's adventures. Although we cannot tell what emotion the figure in the painting is experiencing—whether agony or maenadic frenzy or anger—the power of the heavenly woman is obvious. Jane's world contains God, but—like Charlotte's—it also includes a potentially hostile female presence which looks down on the attempts of a young girl to make her way through this life.

The first painting can be seen as a strange variant of a figure which Brontë had portrayed over and over again since her childhood. Like an Angrian mourner, a cormorant stares at a corpse: "The first represented . . . a swollen sea. [It contained] a half-submerged mast, on which sat a cormorant, dark and large . . . : its beak held a gold bracelet, set with gems. . . . Sinking below the bird and mast, a drowned corpse glanced through the green water; a fair arm was the only limb clearly visible, whence the bracelet had been washed or torn." But two elements are missing from the older Angrian pattern. In the first place, there is no possibility of resurrection implied in Jane's painting. And secondly, the survivor suffers no remorse. Because it is inhuman, the carrion creature need feel no emotion at all. In fact it has stolen the jewels of the dead.

In the plot of the novel, Jane will do her best to avoid the cormorant's crime. She will be horrified when, during their

engagement, she hears that Rochester plans to give her jewelry that once belonged to his mother: "Oh, sir!—never mind
jewels! I don't like to hear them spoken of. Jewels for Jane
Eyre sounds unnatural and strange; I would rather not have
them." And when she finally flees Thornfield, she will leave
behind a symbol of her close brush with sinful audacity: "I
encountered the beads of a pearl necklace Mr. Rochester had
forced me to accept a few days ago. I left that; it was not
mine." To wear fine jewelry, particularly Rochester's family
heirlooms, passed from the dead to the living, would be to
turn a symbol of guilt which the girl has kept hidden in the
recesses of her mind or in cryptic art, into a public badge of
shame. For Jane, as for Charlotte Brontë, survival itself is
apparently a form of grave robbing, a theft of life from the
dead. And thievery ought to be punished.

Punishment is implied in the third painting:

> The third showed the pinnacle of an iceberg piercing a polar
> winter sky: a muster of northern lights reared their dim
> lances, close serried, along the horizon. Throwing these into
> distance, rose, in the foreground, a head,—a colossal head,
> inclined toward the iceberg, and resting against it. Two thin
> hands, joined under the forehead, and supporting it, drew up
> before the lower features a sable veil; a brow quite bloodless,
> white as bone, and an eye hollow and fixed, blank of mean-
> ing but for the glassiness of despair, alone were visible. Above
> the temples . . . gleamed a ring of white flame, gemmed with
> sparkles of a more lurid tinge. This pale crescent was "The
> likeness of a Kingly Crown"; what it diademed was "the
> shape which shape had none."

The Miltonic quotations at the end of the description indicate that Jane sees the picture as an allegorical representation of death. The shapeless shape is Milton's Death, the off-
spring of Sin. But the actual figure in the drawing is,
however distorted, not death but a female mourner—its
sable veil indicates both its gender and the social function in
which it is engaged. Nevertheless, it is entirely possible that,
as in so much of Brontë's art, death really is the child of sin
in this drawing—the sin of the mourner. One cannot say
with certainty that the death of a loved one has sprung from
her sin, but surely the survivor sits in Hell, her head encased
in a ring of white flame, that coalescence of heat and cold
which characterizes the nondialectic union of opposites in
the timeless and unprogressive world of the damned. There
are perhaps guards in the prison in which the woman exists

(the northern lights have lances), but there seems to be no danger of the mourner escaping. For the weight of her depression has chained the woman to her iceberg. In fact she "rests" against it; the iceberg has apparently become a haven of depressive passivity, a familiar if painful cushion against which she leans in quiescent agony. She would apparently not attempt to escape if she could, since her eye, and presumably her mind, are blank of any meaning but despair.

The paintings seem to bring not only Jane, but more importantly Charlotte, out of hiding. Yet they do not present the complete pattern with which *Jane Eyre* is concerned. Death in Jane's paintings is the death of someone else. The paintings do not move forward in time to contemplate the eventual death of the survivor. For emblems of the completed pattern, we have to return to the opening chapters of the novel.

THE TWO FACES OF DEATH

By comparing a book that the little girl studies and a ballad she listens to, we can arrive at the juxtaposition of the two faces of death—death as punishment and death as justification. In the opening chapter of the novel, Jane sits "shrined in double retirement," turning the pages of Bewick's *History of English Birds*. The book reminds her of the nature and the probable outcome of guilt. Jane scans literature for images of the self and its dilemmas. Certainly she finds relevant images in Bewick; her selection of pictures can be seen as a drama projected from her unconscious onto the pages of the book. First she examines the "death-white realms" of northern countries. Throughout the novel she will return again and again to an awed consideration of what it must be like to be dead, to be a spirit in a frozen world. She gazes at a moonlit cemetery, then at two ships which seem like "marine phantoms." The cemetery, like the ships, seems "haunted."

This concentration on the realm of the dead is thoroughly natural for a child whose parents are dead. But Jane does not stop there. Significantly, the images of death and spirits are followed by two pictures which represent crime and punishment. In the first, Jane finds a supernatural avenger of crime, a fiend who has captured a thief by pinning down his booty sack behind him. "'I passed over [that one] quickly: it was an object of terror," Jane remarks. We might legitimately ask at this point what it is that the thief had stolen. Is the sack filled with jewels, perhaps? Jane gives no answer.

We only know that there is a thief who cannot escape the vengeance of a creature from the afterlife. It is perhaps that same thief who is executed in the final picture from Bewick. Jane is terrified by that one, too, frightened by a "black, horned thing seated aloof on a rock, surveying a distant crowd surrounding a gallows."

Jane's taste in books resembles her creator's. The Brontës had been fascinated with Bewick's book during their childhood. The portrayal of the thief and the avenging fiend, in particular, had held their attention for years. Where other children might search the book for robins and sparrows, Charlotte and her heroine find death and apparitions, arrest and execution.

Brontë will allow her protagonist to triumph over the guilt feelings which both she and Jane seem to project onto the pages of the ornithology. To offset the emblems of guilt in the novel, Brontë composes a ballad which treats survival differently. Bewick portrays guilt tracked down; Jane's servant friend Bessie teaches her a song which celebrates the triumph of a persecuted little girl.

SURVIVAL

Death without the inheritance of guilt by the survivor is assumed in the ballad beginning "My feet they are sore, and my limbs they are weary." The survivor is termed "the poor orphan child" and the poem concentrates on her persecution. The child wanders through the moors and rocky hills of a landscape symbolic of pain and isolation. She has been "sent" there, however; she is not fleeing in frightened culpability, like the thief in Bewick, but has been banished because of the cruelty of others. She takes comfort in the knowledge that "kind angels . . . watch o'er" her. Where the supernatural eyes in the bird book had belonged to fiends who watched the shamefaced movements of a criminal, here the lonely child is observed by benign spirits who will take care of her. The orphan is protected by God, who will give her both parentage and an eventual home. But there is a catch: "Heaven is a home, and a rest will not fail me." As in Helen Burns' theology, the entrance fee for the refuge of innocence is death.

In Bewick's book and Bessie's ballad, then, Brontë holds out to her protagonist alternate, sinister explanations of the problem of orphanhood, the problem of survival when loved ones have died. On the one hand, survival might be the result of crime. In that case, death would be a fitting punishment. On the other hand, orphanhood might simply be a martyrdom imposed on an innocent child. If that were true, then perhaps martyrdom ought to be accepted with Christ-like resignation to receive a divine, otherworldly reward.

These two possibilities converge during Jane's imprisonment in the red-room. The complex ambivalence of Charlotte's own attitude toward death seems to be mirrored in the questions Jane asks herself: "What thought had I been but just conceiving of starving myself to death? That certainly was a crime: and was I fit to die? Or was the vault under the chancel of Gateshead Church an inviting bourne?" Brontë's choice of the term "bourne" here is important. It is a word which appears frequently in her writing; she probably associated it above all with one of her favorite books, *Pilgrim's Progress.* In Bunyan's work it refers to the Heavenly City. In *Jane Eyre* it refers ultimately to the goal Jane reaches when she marries Rochester. But for our understanding of the novel, it is important to keep in mind that the first bourne the little girl considers in the novel is the grave. Mr. Reed was her mother's brother and took Jane in after her parents died. Now his ghost might come to take her away: "I thought Mr. Reed's spirit, harassed by the wrongs of his sister's child, might quit its abode—whether in the church vault, or in the unknown world of the departed—and rise before me in this chamber. I wiped my tears and hushed my sobs, fearful lest any sign of violent grief might waken a preternatural voice to comfort me, or elicit from the gloom some haloed face, bending over me with strange pity." Mr. Reed would pity Jane to death. But Jane rebels against receiving comfort from beyond the grave: "I rushed to the door and shook the lock in desperate effort." That desperation is the beginning of wisdom for Jane. *The Professor* had opened with the stern resolve of an adult to become independent. In *Jane Eyre,* Brontë centers on that same motif of independence, but adds to it another dimension—the sometimes frenzied effort of a human being to resist the will to die. The polarity which controlled *The Professor* was success and failure; *Jane Eyre* hovers between life and death, marriage and the grave.

We have dealt so far with isolated scenes and descriptions emblematic of what I believe to be the novel's deepest concerns. But what of the actual story? Surely *Jane Eyre* did not achieve its abiding popularity through a tortured concentration on Charlotte Brontë's personal problems. The novel's striking ability to capture the imagination of its audience has moved more than a century of readers to see themselves mirrored in its heroine. Yet relatively few of those readers can have lost a major portion of their families. *Jane Eyre* is a book for those setting forth into life, not those contemplating death.

A NOVEL ABOUT LIFE

That is precisely the wonderful thing about the novel. There is very little morbidness about the story, or rather we do not *notice* much morbidness on first reading it. For the underlying gloom of the novel's psychological cast is balanced and partially veiled by a narrative which moves toward the light. And it is at least in part the resultant tension between the darkness of Brontë's underlying vision of the world and the surface optimism of the story line which has given so many generations of readers such pleasure.

The story taken in its broad strokes is very nearly a fairy tale, after all. Its movement from darkness to light, from oppression and imprisonment to autonomy and freedom, provides illusory solutions to problems which are not really solvable. But in so doing, the book helps to illuminate the problems. We do not ask of fiction that it solve life's riddles. At most it can show us something about the pressures under which we live, and provide us with a temporary release of our tension. It could be argued that without the naïveté of *Jane Eyre*'s story line, Brontë could not have attained the profundity of the novel's metaphoric drift. Without the existence of illusory, fictive solutions, the problems which tormented her mind would have remained unexpressed, hidden away in the psyche of a woman who, like all of us, would have preferred to avoid them.

The Creation of a Feminist Myth

Helene Moglen

In the following excerpt from her book *Charlotte Brontë: The Self Conceived*, critic Helene Moglen calls *Jane Eyre* Brontë's creation of a feminist myth. According to Moglen, Brontë frees her heroine from the typical dependency and powerlessness associated with femininity: When Jane flees Rochester, and hence the master-student relationship, she rejects women's inferior status and ultimately attains economic independence and self-sufficiency. Jane completes her psychological development when she rejects a sexually repressive relationship with St. John Rivers. Only then, Moglen argues, can the newly liberated and redefined Jane return to the maimed, emasculated, and humbled Rochester.

In deciding to leave Rochester, Jane takes the first crucial step toward independence. She has discovered that there is, after all, something more important to her than pleasing those whom she loves, or giving satisfaction to those who love her. Despite the pain of her conflict, she has acted decisively to preserve her own integrity. At the moment of her decision, Jane returns to the critical scene of her childhood. She is alone in her room as she was alone then—powerless before external circumstances and internal pressures. The limits of the rational world are lost in the boundless universe of imagination:

> That night I never thought to sleep: but a slumber fell on me as soon as I lay down in bed. I was transported in thought to the scenes of childhood: I dreamt I lay in the red-room at Gateshead; that the night was dark, and my mind impressed with strange fears. The light that long ago had struck me into syncope, recalled in this vision, seemed glidingly to mount the wall, and tremblingly to pause in the centre of the ob-

scured ceiling. I lifted up my head to look: the roof resolved to clouds, high and dim; the gleam was such as the moon imparts to vapours she is about to sever. I watched her come—watched with the strangest anticipation; as though some word of doom were to be written on her disk. She broke forth as never moon yet burst from cloud: a hand first penetrated the sable folds and waved them away; then, not a moon, but a white human form shown in the azure, inclining a glorious brow earthward. It gazed and gazed on me. It spoke, to my spirit: immeasureably distant was the tone, yet so near, it whispered in my heart—

"My daughter, flee temptation!"

"Mother, I will."

The terrifying supernatural experience of the red-room is confronted and resolved at last. The strange powers of the nonhuman world seem now but sympathetic extensions of the compelling, equally mysterious forces of the personality. The authority which Jane has sought is female: the moon, maternal nature, the mother within herself—a cosmic and personal principle of order and control.

A VOYAGE OF SELF-DISCOVERY

The trauma at Gateshead had first been neutralized in the experience at Lowood and now, as part of the more profound conflict of Thornfield, is finally resolved. But the antithetical claims which emerged from Jane's relationship with Rochester have still to be reconciled: the needs of the self and the demands of the "other": passion and discipline, egotism and denial. The dialectic proceeds. The first antithesis to Jane's emotionality had been represented by Helen Burns. The second is offered in the more developed and sophisticated form of St. John Rivers. The allegorical movement of self-discovery, present throughout the novel, is intensified here and its Christian structure is emphasized as Jane moves once again into a level of experience that is social and moral rather than personally and sexually defined.

At Lowood Jane was drawn out of the private fantasy world into which she had been thrust by deprivation. Now, after rejecting the romantic idolatry which parallels her childhood experience on another level, she must consciously relocate herself in a complex hierarchy of values: redefining her relationship to God, to nature, to a heterogeneous society previously unknown. She must create a personality independent enough to be separate within the unity of love, secure enough sexually to temper the passion that cloaks self-abnegation. Hers is a radical trial and is expressed through Christian parable.

Fleeing temptation, Jane is set down at Whitcross which "is no town, nor even a hamlet; it is but a stone pillar set up where four roads meet." She is at a beginning and must discover her own way. Like Bunyan's pilgrim, Christian, she is bereft of friends and family: homeless and penniless. She must be purged of all human vanity, enduring the humiliation of body and spirit. At first she finds comfort in the maternal nature which had always before offered her solace:

> Nature seemed to me benign and good: I thought she loved me, outcast that I was; and I, who from man could anticipate only mistrust, rejection, insult, clung to her with filial fondness. Tonight, at least, I would be her guest—as I was her child: my mother would lodge me without money and without price.

But although she, like all men and women, is related to the natural world, she is not truly a part of it:

> What a golden desert this spreading moor! Everywhere sunshine. I wished I could live in it and on it. I saw a lizard run over the crag; I saw a bee busy among the sweet bilberries. I would fain at the moment have become bee or lizard, that I might have found fitting nutriment, permanent shelter here. But I was a human being, and had a human being's wants: I must not linger where there was nothing to supply them.

God, the Father, had given and secured her life. The only mother she can look to in her present trouble is the mother within. She had discovered her presence on the evening of the departure from Thornfield. Now she must test her power:

> Life, however, was yet in my possession; with all its requirements, and pains, and responsibilities. The burden must be carried; the want provided for; the suffering endured: the responsibility fulfilled. I set out.

At Lowood, hunger seemed in part to be experienced as a need for love. Now the mature Jane confronts similar but more pressing deprivations—starvation and death from exposure. Both are spiritual as well as physical trials. She must again discover and assert the self that can endure. Despite privation (reduced to eating pig's food, brought to a state of beggary) Jane is able to retain a degree of pride appropriate to a character strengthened by the resolve of independent choice and action. And that pride is also softened by new sympathy for those who must, as she, endure the humbling miseries of existence.

MARSH END

Finally, at the point of death, Jane follows a light which leads her to Marsh End, a sanctuary of civilization poised at the edge of the wild, open moors. Looking through the window into the scrupulously clean and pleasant kitchen, she sees an elderly female servant and "two young, graceful women—ladies in every point," one with a dog's head resting on her knee, one with a kitten curled in her lap. Busily involved in their translation of German, they are indeed images of "delicacy and cultivation." First denied entrance by the servant, Hannah, Jane is finally admitted by St. John Rivers, the brother of Diana and Mary. Her ordeal is ended. She sleeps for three days and three nights, waking only to eat and drink of the food and water of life. Her sleep renews her spirit as it restores her body and is reminiscent of the crisis that followed her ordeal in the red-room. Her first act after awakening is her forgiveness of Hannah for denying her shelter. She cautions this impotent surrogate for the wicked parent that "Some of the best people that ever lived have been as destitute as I am; and if you are a Christian, you ought not to consider poverty a crime." Her clasping of Hannah's hand marks her entrance into the Christian community and her acceptance of social interrelatedness.

Jane had before found comfort and definition in the female environment at Lowood. Now, after completely identifying with Rochester, it is crucial for her to discover herself anew in the images of women. Through her friendship with Diana and Mary Rivers, she becomes stronger, more confident, more focused. In them, free as they are of dependence upon men, strong in their devotion to one another, she finds the form of a new promise of fulfillment. She shares with them their love of nature. She admires and respects their superior learning, their fine minds. She listens to them talk as she had once listened to Maria Temple and Helen Burns, as Charlotte had listened to Emily and Anne. She responds to the authority in Diana—with her it is natural to be passive, "feminine," "to bend where my conscience and self-respect permitted, to an active will." But there is still equality among them. No longer functioning within the authoritarian context of the master-student relationship she had with Rochester, she finds instead that there can be intellectual reciprocity: a sharing of knowledge and gifts, delight in the interaction of personalities. The strength and confidence which she derives from their friendship allows her to accept the job which St. John offers her as teacher in the village school. Assuming this role, she begins to overcome her feelings of social humiliation:

> I felt desolate to a degree. I felt—yes, idiot that I am—I felt degraded. I doubted I had taken a step which sank instead of raising me in the scale of social existence. I was weakly dismayed at the ignorance, the poverty, the coarseness of all I heard and saw round me. But let me not hate and despise myself too much for these feelings: I know them to be wrong—that is a great step gained; I shall strive to overcome them.

And she does largely overcome them (although Jane Eyre, as Charlotte Brontë herself, could not be accused of excessive egalitarian tendencies). She discovers in many of her poor and unlearned students a degree of "natural politeness" and "innate self-respect'" which wins her good will and admiration. She takes pride in her accomplishment, in her ability to teach and befriend her students, to be self-sufficient and useful. And her success earns her a position in the little community so that it is enjoyable for her "to live amidst general regard, though it be but the regard of working-people."

The tone of *noblesse oblige* which informs these words provides us with some understanding of the direction which Charlotte Brontë's myth must take. Feminist it might well be, but it is not a feminism which can preach or envision radical social change. Jane, in leaving Rochester, must, it is true, discover her own capacities and strengths. She must learn the pleasures of independence and self-sufficiency. But only economic independence and social position will give her the status essential to the recognition which is the better part of equality.

KINSHIP AND FORTUNE

When St. John informs her of her sizable inheritance and of the fact that he and his sisters are her real cousins, Jane realizes immediately the way in which her life will now be changed. "It was a grand boon doubtless; and independence would be glorious—yes, I felt that—*that* thought swelled my heart." She recognizes also that by sharing her wealth with Diana and Mary she can free them as she herself is now freed, from the dreary servitude of work. She will have with them "a home and connections" and she will be liberated from the necessity of marrying where there is no love.

Discovering her kinship with the Riverses, Jane does, of course follow in the tradition of the heroes and heroines of quest-romance. Social recognition validates internal worth. The implication is that class membership is its very condition. A "lady" is born, not made, even though the secret of her birth might remain hidden. The Riverses are the last of the series of families to which Jane has found herself intimately or distantly connected. In structure they resemble the Reeds and the Ingrams. All have two daughters (Jane stands outside as a stepsister) and a son. The fathers are dead, the mothers living (Hannah is a kindly, unthreatening, surrogate-mother for the Rivers children as Tabby was for the Brontës). But all the earlier families are "bad" or "false." As indications of the incompleteness of Jane's development, they have signaled successive stages of her "'trial": a continuing inability to confront a self that has been "earned." It is with her "real" family that Jane shares her birthright, joyously seizing "the delicious pleasure of which I have caught a glimpse—that of repaying, in part, a mighty obligation, and winning to myself lifelong friends." Here is the multi-layered magic of fairy tale. Jane is transformed from stepsister to benefactress. This is the role which Charlotte was to play with her sisters; which she would have wished to play with [her brother] Branwell, had he been less threatening.

Significantly, it is St. John who pushes her to further recognition of possibility; to further discoveries of herself. He must be the agent of her liberation. If Rochester represents one aspect of Jane's personality, St. John represents the other. On one level, it is the conflict between Byron and the duke of Wellington articulated with psychological subtlety. St. John Rivers is an older and, more importantly, a masculine version of Helen Burns. Without innocence, or naiveté, he is purposeful, directed, threatening. In both of them the spiritual impulse is carried to an extreme: a form of sublimation which can be liberating and creative, but can also destroy.

St. John's Grecian appearance identifies him with the classical virtues of reason and control so admired in *Rasselas*. He is fair and pale, his light is repressed and "burns" as Helen's did, within. While the fire of the red-room and the fire of the wild, impassioned Berthe threaten destruction to others, St. John's fire is, as Jane sees, self-consuming.

PLAIN JANE

At first glance, Jane Eyre *is an unlikely heroine; she is
poor, plain, and self-effacing. In her biography* The Life of
Charlotte Brontë, *Elizabeth Gaskell explains why the novelist
refused to portray a beautiful and charming Jane.*

[Charlotte Brontë] once told her sisters that they were wrong
—even morally wrong—in making their heroines beautiful as
a matter of course. They replied that it was impossible to
make a heroine interesting on any other terms. Her answer
was, 'I will prove to you that you are wrong; I will show you a
heroine as plain and as small as myself, who shall be as interesting as any of yours.' Hence Jane Eyre . . .

Elizabeth Gaskell, *The Life of Charlotte Brontë,* 1924.

. . . that heart is already laid on a sacred altar: the fire is
arranged round it. It will soon be no more than a sacrifice
consumed.

In him, Charlotte Brontë has drawn a stunning portrait of the
martyr—unsoftened by the childish idealism or female vul-
nerability which made Helen sympathetic. Defining self-
denial as it own virtue, St. John wishes to sacrifice his life to
others although he is, by his own admission, a "cold, hard
man."

He subscribes, as Helen did, to a Calvinism that is bitter
and stern, full of the promise of guilt and punishment. But
he identifies himself with the punishing authority of that religion, casting himself as avenging angel rather than as victim. He has found in the missionary's calling a way of chan-
neling his ambitions as soldier, statesman, orator: "a lover of
renown, a luster after power," and he brings to his "profes-
sion" the hardness and despotism that befit a man of the
world. His sadistic arrogance is the male version of Helen's
masochism.

Charlotte Brontë describes St. John as "a cold, cumbrous,
column." She had used a similar image for Brocklehurst
who was "a black pillar . . . a straight, narrow, sable-clad
shape." The identification of male sexuality and power on
one hand and that same sexuality with rigidity—even
death—on the other, is hardly accidental. The extent to
which St. John purchases his religious calling at the cost of
sexual passion is illustrated in his abortive relationship
with Rosamond Oliver, the charming girl whom he rejects

precisely because he is attracted to her. And the extent to which his religious fervor is the result of sexual fear and repression is revealed in his more subtle and complex relationship with Jane.

JANE'S TEMPTATION

He is attracted to Jane initially because of her courage in adversity. Knowing her past, he is familiar with the strength of her moral fiber. In her attention to her students he sees that she is diligent, orderly, and energetic as well as intelligent. He recognizes in her desire to share her inheritance, a gift for sacrifice, and he feels in her response to him an appropriate recognition of his power. For these reasons, he concludes that she would make him a useful helpmate. But there is an enormous contradiction in his attitude toward her. He does not want to see her as a woman. He would, in fact, have her deny her sexual nature, her feelings, her body—subordinate that which is most vital in her self to his own spiritual quest. Her passivity and masochism respond to him:

> As for me, I daily wished more to please him: but to do so, I felt daily more and more that I must disown half my nature, stifle my faculties, wrest my tastes from their original bent, force myself to the adoption of pursuits for which I had no natural vocation. He wanted to train me to an elevation I could never reach: it racked me hourly to aspire to the standard he uplifted.

The great problem arises from his insistence that she must join him in his missionary labors, not as a friend, not as a "sister," but as a wife: "A sister might any day be taken from me. I want a wife: a soul helpmeet I can influence efficiently in life and retain absolutely till death." He wants to control her completely. For Jane the temptation is strong. Commitment to the work, even to the death which she sees as the inevitable outcome of her existence: this would focus her life and obscure her love for Rochester by employing her physical and intellectual energies. She is willing to defy society and sacrifice her life to participate in that larger mission in which she can only partially believe. It is possible to compromise worldly interests and spiritual doubts, but she cannot sacrifice her sexuality. And there is no question that her sexuality is at issue.

St. John's manipulative power, the loftiness of his aspirations, the largeness of his will—all evoke a response based upon her habitual tendency to submit to a dominating spirit, her need for approval and respect.

> By degrees he acquired a certain influence over me that took away my liberty of mind: his praise and notice were more restraining than his indifference.

The attraction Jane feels is not unrelated to the idolatry of her love for Rochester. It is that aspect of sexuality which is power-oriented, potentially sadomasochistic:

> . . . Though I have only sisterly affection for him now, yet, if forced to be his wife, I can imagine the possibility of conceiving an inevitable, strange, torturing kind of love for him: because he is so talented; and there is often a certain heroic grandeur in his look, manner and conversation.

Jane recognizes that St. John would buy her body with the coin of spirituality, hypocritically posing as God's agent. "Do you think God will be satisfied with half an oblation?" he asks her. "Will he accept a mutilated sacrifice? It is the cause of God I advocate: it is under His standard I enlist you." St. John must make a religious duty of sexual need. He explicitly denies his own and therefore her sexuality, fearing the passion which would make him mortal and vulnerable. As she comes to understand St. John, Jane is so distressed by his twisted, sadistic (albeit unconscious) misrepresentation of his own feeling and by his misunderstanding of hers that she angrily and openly opposes him. When he says: "Undoubtedly enough of love would follow upon marriage to render the union right even in your eyes," she replies: "I scorn your idea of love . . . I scorn the counterfeit sentiment you offer: yes, St. John, and I scorn you when you offer it." It is the extraordinary contempt of a virginal young woman for the Victorian concept of sex as duty, for the Victorian denial of the dignity of human passion. But there still remains in Jane the other side of that Victorian repression: the overwhelming desire to submit to a power that will envelope her, possess her, negate her.

> I was tempted to cease struggling with him—to rush down the torrent of his will into the gulf of his existence, and there lose my own.

Well might she say, "I was almost as hard beset by him now as I had been once before, in a different way, by another."

SEXUAL IMAGERY

In the final scene between Jane and St. John, the language of spiritual transfiguration is interlaced with the language and

imagery of sexuality. The images of the red-room are re-
called as well as the dreams that preceded Jane's decision at
Thornfield:

> I stood motionless under my hierophant's touch. My refusals
> were forgotten—my fears overcome—my wrestlings para-
> lyzed. The Impossible—i.e. my marriage with St. John—was
> fast becoming the Possible. All was changing utterly, with a
> sudden sweep. Religion called—Angels beckoned—God com-
> manded—life rolled together like a scroll—death's gates
> opening, shewed eternity beyond: it seemed, that for safety
> and bliss there, all here might be sacrificed in a second. The
> dim room was full of visions.

> The one candle was dying out: the room was full of moon-
> light. My heart beat fast and thick: I heard its throb. Suddenly
> it stood still to an inexpressible feeling that thrilled it through,
> and passed at once to my head and extremities. The feeling
> was not like an electric shock; but it was quite as sharp, as
> strange, as startling: it acted on my senses as if their utmost
> activity hitherto had been but torpor; from which they were
> now summoned, and forced to wake.

Two other profound psychic experiences had occasioned the
fear of loss and violation sufficiently terrifying to induce un-
consciousness. This third time, much strengthened, Jane is
impelled to self-assertive action. Now she is released by orgasmic convulsion into spiritual resolution and sexual re-
definition. The response is summoned by the sexual compo-
nent of St. John's power, but it yields awareness and self
discovery instead of dread annihilation. Much of the dangerous appeal of Rochester's sexuality had derived from a
similar charisma of power (a charisma not completely lacking, as masculine force, even in Brocklehurst and John
Reed). That appeal is experienced here fully—and finally,
absolutely rejected. (Not least of all, the brother-lover is implicitly rejected, literally "sacrificed," as we later learn, in favor of the lover-husband.) Now Jane is free to explore the
potential that remains. When she hears Rochester's voice
calling to her, she responds as surely to the need it expresses
as she responds to the need in herself which she must acknowledge. Rather than accepting the sublimation of desire
in a patriarchial religious value system, she finds spiritual
meaning in human experience. She rejects sexual passion
that derives its force from masochistic self-denial and insists
that duty and obligation must be placed within the context of
a generous and reciprocal human love.

In rejecting St. John, Jane comes to terms with her need

for an external authority. She completes the move toward independence begun in the red-room and continued in her departure from Thornfield. In rejecting St. John's repressive sexuality she rejects the perverse sadomasochism it implies, and she attempts to distinguish the sexuality of love from the sexuality of power: the love born of equality from the love subject to idolatry.

This is the last of the symbolic "separations." At every previous point of parting (from Bessie, Helen, Maria Temple, Rochester) Jane's "self," apparently severed and divided, has become stronger and more integrated than before. The separation from St. John marks the ultimate resolution of her spiritual and sexual being, but the transformation of the Edward Rochester to whom she returns is the crucial condition of the actualization of that being and therefore of the viability of the new romantic myth which the novel has articulated.

ROLE REVERSAL

In her return to Thornfield, Jane is as little motivated by moral considerations as she had been before in her departure. She is driven by premonition and passion rather than principle or judgment.

> Could I but see him! Surely, in that case, I should not be so mad as to run to him? I cannot tell—I am not certain. And if I did—what then? God bless him! What then? Who would be hurt by my once more tasting the life his glance can give me?

She finds Thornfield in ruins: destroyed by the mystery of fire and blood which had been secreted within it for so long: set aflame by Berthe, who was killed while attempting to escape from her husband. The house is the very image of its former master who, Samson-like, maddened by loneliness, desperate and trapped within the futility of his rebellion, had pulled his home down about himself, blinded and crippled his body, deprived himself of that which he had most valued and most feared: the power and pride of his "masculinity." The ambivalence of the Byronic hero towards his own sexuality is nowhere better expressed than in Rochester's attempted rescue of his mad wife, described to Jane by one of the townspeople:

> I witnessed, and several more witnessed Mr. Rochester ascend through the skylight to the roof; we heard him call "Berthe!" We saw him approach her; and then, ma'am, she yelled, and gave a spring, and the next minute she lay smashed on the pavement.

The saviour appears to the victim as avenger and rescue it-self becomes a kind of murder. Rochester's heroism, not un-like Byron's own, is realized in self-destruction.

Jane seeking Rochester at Ferndean reminds us paradox-ically—yet justly—of the Prince who comes to awaken the sleeping Beauty with a kiss. Their roles are now reversed. All is dark and overgrown, the decaying house buried in the gloomy, tangled forest as Rochester's spirit is hidden in his broken body. Watching him emerge, Jane thinks "of some wronged and fettered wild-beast or bird, dangerous to ap-proach in his sullen woe . . . the caged eagle, whose gold-ringed eyes cruelty has extinguished." That she had in past times reminded him of a small, helpless bird trapped in a nest metaphorizes our sense of their role reversal.

Brontë has afflicted her hero with the Christian punish-ment appropriate to one who has "committed adultery in his heart" and "put aside his wife." It is the punishment proph-esied earlier by Jane in the first agony of her discovery of Rochester's wife.

> You shall, yourself, pluck out your right eye; yourself cut off your right hand: your heart shall be the victim; and you, the priest, to transfix it.

And the punishment is appropriate in far more subtle ways as well: in ways which speak to the social, psychological, and sexual disease of which "romantic love" is a symptom. In the cost to Rochester of the resolution of Jane's conflict, the severity of social and psychological pressures are most painfully demonstrated. Just as Henry Hastings's disintegra-tion was essential to Elizabeth's discovery of her own abili-ties and as Charlotte's personal and artistic growth were predicated upon both Branwell's moral and physical col-lapse and [her father] Patrick Brontë's increasing depen-dence, so too can Jane's development be maintained only at the cost of Rochester's romantic self-image. Rochester's mu-tilation is, in the terms of this nascent feminist myth, the necessary counterpart of Jane's independence: the terrible condition of a relationship of equality.

But what, in fact, is the nature of this "equality?" Jane's flight from the orgasmic knowledge of St. John's sexual power and Rochester's last catastrophic struggle with his vampire-bride are not the bases of a mature sexuality which is an extension of social liberation. They are rather preludes to the desexualization which is the unhappy compromise necessary when psychosexual need is unsupported by social reality or political self-consciousness. The mystery of fire and blood is not solved. It is simply eradicated. Jane's sense of Rochester, as she looks at him on the morning after her return, is crucial:

> His countenance reminded one of a lamp quenched, waiting to be relit—and alas! it was not himself that could kindle the lustre of animated expression: he was dependent on another for that office.

He is devitalized; the fire of his passion burnt to ash; the quick of his nature paralyzed. He is not the bereaved lover, expectantly awaiting his mistress's return. His is a comatose soul, unable to cry out for rebirth. It is not a lover he requires, but a mother who can offer him again the gift of life. And it is this function which Jane will gratefully assume.

> I love you better now, when I can really be useful to you, than I did in your state of proud independence, when you disdained every part but that of the giver and protector.

Brontë, dividing her time between the writing of her novel and the nursing of her weak and sightless father, could well have spoken these words with Jane. They belong to the virginal daughter who has been magically transformed—without the mediation of sexual contact—into the noble figure of the nurturing mother. Once the magical transformation has taken place, the dependence defined, the partial restoration of Rochester's vision cannot reverse the pattern of relationship any more easily than the removal of Patrick Brontë's cataracts could completely reestablish the old patriarchal order.

ROCHESTER'S TRANSFORMATION

Jane's money and social status, even her confidence and self-knowledge, would not have offered her sufficient protection against the psychosexual power of Rochester, her "master"; would not have defended her against the arrogance and pride supported by society through its laws, its structures, its attitudes, its mythology. Nor would her new position, her developed self, have protected Rochester from the fears and actual dangers associated with the "masculine" role assigned to him. So strong are these external forces that the reduction of Rochester's virility and the removal of them both from contact with society are necessary to maintain the integrity of the emergent female self Rochester is brought into the "female" word of love and morality, out of the "masculine" universe of power: out of society, into Jane's sphere of psychic functioning. His transformation heralds the death of the Byronic hero whose many charms were the imaginative instruments of a sexually repressive and oppressive society. But the society into which his maimed Victorian spirit is reborn, is still more repressive and more closed. Brontë's myth reflects those social limitations even as it attempts to define a new feminist freedom. Rochester is, in this sense, a pivotal figure; marking the transition from the romantic to the modern hero, heralding the paralyzing alienation which will be chronicled by Dickens, by Thackeray, by George Eliot, and Lawrence: by Melville, by Mann, by Kafka, and Dostoevsky. His mangled body projects his psychic scars. His absence of vitality derives from a psychic illness which will become, in many of his successors, spiritual death.

Rochester is the representative and victim of forces over which Jane has triumphed in order to redefine herself. But the self which emerges from the sequential struggles it endures cannot be tested again by former adversaries. The allegorical quest follows a necessary and irreversible path. In its victories, the ego absorbs those components of reality which it has successfully confronted, negating their existence as objective form. The aggressive, even sadistic "masculinity" of John Reed, and Brocklehurst, of St. John and the younger Rochester are all contained within the humbled and broken hero whom Jane ultimately nourishes and sustains. This is, of course, the fantasy element of Brontë's feminist myth. It would not be for almost fifty years that social change and aroused political consciousness would make it possible to test an awareness and achievement like Jane Eyre's against realistic pressures. In England it would not be until the twentieth century and the fiction of D.H. Lawrence that the descendents of the maimed Rochester and the liberated Jane would be able to face each other in the full complexity of their social, sexual, and psychological conflicts. In our own time we struggle still to break through the irrational identification of phallic potency with political, social, and economic domination.

There is, in the naive resolution of *Jane Eyre*, an idealization of Jane and Rochester's life together which is part of the logic of the psychosexual romance. The last chapter begins with an extraordinary statement that places Jane at the center of the relationship. "Reader, I married him," she says and continues:

I have now been married ten years. I know what it is to live entirely for and with what I love best on earth. I hold myself supremely blest—blest beyond what language can express; because I am my husband's life as fully as he is mine. No woman was ever nearer to her mate than I am: absolutely more bone of his bone, and flesh of his flesh. I know no weariness of my Edward's society: he knows none of mine, any more than we do of the pulsation of the heart that beats in our separate bosoms; consequently, we are ever together. To be together is for us to be at once as free as in solitude, as gay as in company. We talk, I believe, all day long: to talk to each other is but an animated and audible thinking. All my confidence is bestowed on him; all his confidence is devoted to me: we are precisely suited in character; perfect concord is the result.

But the truth of this relationship is an interior truth, as remote from social reality as are Gateshead, Lowood, Thornfield, Marsh End, and Ferndean—themselves all landscapes of psychological development. It is the truth of Charlotte Brontë's dream that we have here: the truth of her fantasy. To the extent that it dramatizes the conflict of larger social and psychological forces, it offers also the larger truth of myth. But what is extraordinary is that this novel, born of repression and frustration, of limited experience and less hope, should have offered an insight into psychosexual relationships that was visionary in its own time and remains active in ours.

Ambiguity in *Jane Eyre*

Terry Eagleton

According to Terry Eagleton, *Jane Eyre* is a vehicle by which Brontë questions the social order and explores spiritual equality and an individual's quest for independence. All of Brontë's novels, Eagleton claims, "dramatize a society in which all human relationships are power struggles," and ambiguity about power, specifically, is a recurrent theme of *Jane Eyre*. Hence Jane craves a complex blend of equality, independence, and—paradoxically—subservience to a superior will. Eagleton is the author of *Myths of Power: A Marxist Study of the Brontës*, from which the following is excerpted.

At the centre of all Charlotte's novels, I am arguing, is a figure who either lacks or deliberately cuts the bonds of kinship. This leaves the self a free, blank, 'pre-social' atom: free to be injured and exploited, but free also to progress, move through the class-structure, choose and forge relationships, strenuously utilise its talents in scorn of autocracy or paternalism. The novels are deeply informed by this bourgeois ethic, but there is more to be said than that. For the social status finally achieved by the *déraciné* self, is at once meritoriously won and inherently proper. Jane's uncle is said to be a tradesman, and the Reeds despise her for it; but Bessie comments that the Eyres were as much gentry as the Reeds, and her Rivers cousins have an impressively ancient lineage. Rochester seems a grander form of gentry, and Jane's relationship with him is of course socially unequal; but it is, nevertheless, a kind of returning home as well as an enviable move upwards. Given relationships are certainly constrictive: they mediate a suave violence deep-seated in society itself, as John Reed's precociously snobbish remark suggests. But knowing where you genetically belong still counts for a good deal in the end. Charlotte's fiction portrays

the unprotected self in its lonely conquest of harsh conditions, and so intimates a meritocratic vision; but individual-
ist self-reliance leads you to roles and relations which are
objectively fitting.

Jane, then, disowns what second-hand kin she has, caring
never to see the Reeds again, surviving instead by her own
talents; she creates the relationships which matter, those of
spiritual rather than blood affinity. ('I believe [Rochester] is
of mine;—I am sure he is,—I feel akin to him . . . though
rank and wealth sever us widely, I have something in my
brain and heart, in my blood and nerves, that assimilates me
mentally to him.') Spiritual affinity, indeed, is more physical
and full-blooded than the icy *rapport* one has with literal
kinsfolk like Rivers. In this as in other ways, however, Jane
is granted the best of both worlds. Just as her resources for
solitary survival run out, on the long exhausting flight from
Thornfield, she is supplied with a new set of kinsfolk who
turn out this time to be pleasant. The Rivers sisters provide
a cultivated retreat into which Jane can temporarily relax;
she rests her head on Diana's lap in delighted gratitude at
her discovery of blood-relations, even though the event will
prove merely a stopping-off place *en route* to the grander
gentility of Rochester. This time, however, her relation to
kinsfolk is not that of servile dependence. On the contrary, it
is they who are now in part dependent on her: each of them
gets a quarter share of her newfound wealth. The legacy allows Jane to combine sturdy independence with a material
sealing of her affinity with others. Given relationships are
good, if you may negotiate them on your own terms; kins-
men are both gift and threat. It is an ambivalence reflected
in Jane's feelings towards Mrs Reed: she upbraids her hotly
for neglecting familial duty, but curiously excuses that brutality by wondering 'how could she really like an interloper
not of her race, and unconnected with her, after her husband's death, by any tie?' Whether 'race' matters or not
seems a moot point in Jane's own mind.

SPIRITUAL EQUALITY

Jane's relative isolation from given relationships results in
a proud autonomy of spirit, one which in some ways implicitly questions the class-structure. She has too much self-
respect to lavish her love on an unresponsive Rochester:
'He is not of your order; keep to your caste; and be too self-

respecting to lavish the love of the whole heart, soul, and
strength, where such a gift is not wanted and may be de-
spised.' Yet the comment, of course, endorses the class-
structure as well as suggesting the spiritual inferiority of
one's betters: if the callously insensitive aristocrat cannot
recognise a gift when he sees one, then it is wise to remain
self-righteously on one's own side of the social divide. In so
far as it is for him to make the overture, Jane's attitude combines deference with independence; yet 'independence' is a
thoroughly ambiguous term. It means not wanting to be a
servant, which implies a class-judgement on those below
you as well as suggesting a radical attitude to those above.
Jane's rebellion against the Reeds engages certain egalitarian feelings: she rejects the idea of paternalist benefaction as
disagreeable, and later values her equal relationship with
Mrs Fairfax for the freedom it brings. 'The equality between
her and me was real; not the mere result of condescension
on her part; so much the better—my position was all the
freer.' But independence in this society involves attaining a
precarious gentility (Bessie has to admit that the adult Jane
is now, at least, a lady), and that in turn entails a sharp eye
for the nuance of social distinction. Jane is furious with the
Reeds because they treat her as a servant when she isn't
one; her smouldering hatred of their snobbery is thus shot
through with shared class-assumptions about the poor. ('No;
I should not like to belong to poor people.') Her response to
the pupils at Morton school is similarly double-edged: distasteful though she finds their unmannerliness, she 'must
not forget that these coarsely-clad little peasants are of flesh
and blood as good as the scions of the gentlest genealogy;
and that the germs of native excellence, refinement, intelligence, kind feeling, are as likely to exist in their hearts as in
those of the best born'. The demotic generosity of this is
sharply qualified by that stern self-reminder; Jane's doctrine
of spiritual equality stems logically from her own experience, but it has to fight hard against the social discrimina-
tions bred into an expensively clad child. (Her egalitarian
defence of the 'British peasantry' is based, ironically, on a
dogma of chauvinist superiority: they are at least preferable
to their 'ignorant, coarse, and besotted' European counter-
parts.) Jane feels degraded by her role as schoolmistress ('I
had taken a step which sank instead of raising me in the
scale of social existence'), but guiltily scorns the feeling as

'idiotic'; and that tension deftly defines the petty-bourgeois consciousness which clings to real class-distinctions while spiritually rejecting them. She is, for instance, priggishly quick to point out to the Rivers' servant Hannah that she may be a beggar but at least she is a high-class one:

'Are you book-learned?' [Hannah] inquired, presently.

'Yes, very.'

The snobbish Hannah must be given an object-lesson in social equality, taught not to judge by appearances, so Jane reveals how superior she is to the old woman. Even in beggary class counts: St John Rivers, presumably noting Jane's refined accent when Hannah turns her from his door, surmises instantly that this is a 'peculiar case'. Jane's insistence on getting past the servant and appealing to the young ladies glimpsed within is, indeed, sound class tactics: the sisters are presented as idealised versions of herself, quiet, spiritual and self-composed.

Jane's relationship with Rochester is marked by these ambiguities of equality, servitude and independence. He himself conceives of the union in terms of spiritual equality: '"My bride is here", he said, again drawing me to him, "because my equal is here, and my likeness. Jane, will you marry me?"' Far from offering a radically alternative ethic, spiritual equality is what actually smooths your progress through the class-system; Rochester may be spiritually egalitarian but he is still socially eligible. Jane is on the whole submissive to social hierarchy but shares her master's view that spiritual qualities count for more: she has no hesitation in dismissing Blanche Ingram as inferior to herself. She wants a degree of independence in marriage—'"It would indeed be a relief", I thought, "if I had ever so small an independency"'—but it is, significantly, 'small': she can hope to bring Rochester an accession of fortune but hardly to get on genuinely equal terms. Independence, then, is an intermediate position between complete equality and excessive docility: it allows you freedom, but freedom within a proper deference.

Dominance and Submission

When stung to righteous anger, Jane can certainly claim a fundamental human equality with her employer: 'Do you think, because I am poor, obscure, plain, and little, I am soulless and heartless?' There are, in fact, reasons other than simple humanitarian ones why Jane and Rochester are not as socially divided as may at first appear. Rochester, the younger son of an avaricious landed gentleman, was denied his share in the estate and had to marry instead into colonial wealth; Jane's colonial uncle dies and leaves her a sizeable legacy, enough for independence. The colonial trade which signified a decline in status for Rochester signifies an advance in status for Jane, so that although they are of course socially unequal, their fortunes spring from the same root. Yet Jane does not finally claim equality with Rochester; the primary terms on which Charlotte Brontë's fiction handles relationships are those of dominance and submission. The novels dramatise a society in which almost all human relationships are power-struggles; and because 'equality' therefore comes to be defined as equality of power, it is an inevitably complicated affair. Jane serves in the end 'both for [Rochester's] prop and guide', which is an interestingly ambiguous situation. It suggests subservience, and so perpetuates their previous relationship; but the subservience is also, of course, a kind of leadership. Whether she likes it or not, Jane finally comes to have power over Rochester. Her ultimate relation to him is a complex blend of independence (she comes to him on her own terms, financially self-sufficient), submissiveness, and control.

This complex blend is a recurrent feature of relationships in the novels. Charlotte's protagonists want independence, but they also desire to dominate; and their desire to dominate is matched only by their impulse to submit to a superior will. The primary form assumed by this ambiguity is a sexual one: the need to venerate and revere, but also to exercise power, enacts itself both in a curious rhythm of sexual attraction and antagonism, and in a series of reversals of sexual roles. The maimed and blinded Rochester, for example, is in an odd way even more 'masculine' than he was before (he is 'brown', 'shaggy', 'metamorphosed into a lion'), but because he is helpless he is also 'feminine' (A sexual ambiguity prefigured in Rochester's masquerading as an old gypsy woman. Then he was a masculine female, now he is a feminine male.); and Jane, who adopts a traditionally feminine role towards him ('It is time some one undertook to rehumanise you'), is thereby forced into the male role of protectiveness. She finds him both attractive and ugly, as he finds her both plain and fascinating. Rochester's lack of conventional good looks, in contrast to Rivers's blandly classical features, reflects his idiosyncratic roughness and so underlines his male mastery, but it also makes him satisfyingly akin to Jane herself. Blanche Ingram is a 'beauty', but her aggressive masculinity contrasts sharply with Jane's pale subduedness; her dominative nature leads her to desire a husband who will be a foil rather than a rival to her, but it also prompts her to despise effeminate men and admire strong ones:

> 'I grant an ugly *woman* is a blot on the fair face of creation; but as to the *gentlemen*, let them be solicitous to possess only strength and valour: let their motto be: —Hunt, shoot and fight: the rest is not worth a fillip. Such should be my device, were I a man.'

> 'Whenever I marry,' she continued, after a pause which none interrupted, 'I am resolved my husband shall not be a rival, but a foil to me. I will suffer no competitor near the throne; I shall exact an undivided homage; his devotions shall not be shared between me and the shape he sees in his mirror.'

The arrogance of this, of course, counts heavily against Blanche; it is hardly likely to charm the listening Rochester. Jane, who shares Blanche's liking for 'devilish' men, knows better than she does how they are to be handled—when to exert her piquant will and when to be cajolingly submissive:

> I knew the pleasure of vexing and soothing him by turns; it was one I chiefly delighted in, and a sure instinct always prevented me from going too far: beyond the verge of provocation I never ventured; on the extreme brink I liked well to try my skill. Retaining every minute form of respect, every propriety of my station, I could still meet him in argument without fear or uneasy restraint: this suited both him and me.

Jane moves deftly between male and female roles in her courtship of Rochester; unlike Blanche, who is tall, dark and dominating like Rochester himself, she settles astutely for a vicarious expression of her own competitive maleness through him. She preserves the proprieties while turning them constantly to her advantage, manipulating convention for both self-protection and self-advancement.

AMBIGUITY ABOUT POWER

This simultaneity of attraction and antagonism, reverence and dominance, is relevant to a more general ambiguity about power which pervades Charlotte's fiction. It parallels and embodies the conflicting desires of the oppressed outcast for independence, for passive conformity to a secure social order, and for avenging self-assertion over that order. Revenge does not, in fact, seem too strong a word for what happens at the end of *Jane Eyre*. Jane's repressed indignation at a dominative society, prudently swallowed back throughout the book, is finally released—not by Jane herself, but by the novelist; and the victim is the symbol of that social order, Rochester. The crippled Rochester is the novel's sacrificial offering to social convention, to Jane's subconscious hostility and, indeed, to her own puritan guilt; by satisfying all three demands simultaneously, it allows her to adopt a suitably subjugated role while experiencing a fulfilling love and a taste of power. Jane's guilt about Rochester's passion and her own is strikingly imaged in the grotesque figure of Bertha: the Bertha who tries on Jane's wedding veil is a projection of Jane's sexually tormented subconsciousness, but since Bertha is masculine, black-visaged and almost the same height as her husband, she appears also as a repulsive symbol of Rochester's sexual drive. The point of the novel's conclusion is to domesticate that drive so that it ceases to be minatory while remaining attractive. In the end, the outcast bourgeoise achieves more than a humble place at the fireside: she also gains independence vis-à-vis the upper class, and the right to engage in the process of taming it. The worldly Rochester has already been purified by fire; it is now for Jane to rehumanise him. By the device of an ending, bourgeois initiative and genteel settlement. sober rationality and Romantic passion, spiritual equality and social distinction, the actively affirmative and the patiently deferential self, can be merged into mythical unity.

The Nature of Love and Marriage in *Jane Eyre*

Martin S. Day

The unsophisticated yet passionate Jane must choose between the romantic but flawed Rochester—who is incompatible with Jane except in love—and the noble but cold St. John Rivers, who by all outward appearances is an exemplary match for Jane. In his psychological reading of Jane's dilemma, Martin S. Day analyzes Jane's motives in eschewing both a grossly unequal liaison with Rochester and a loveless union with Rivers. Day, a professor of English, has contributed articles to several journals, including the following critical analysis, which appeared in *The Personalist.*

From the earliest reviews of *Jane Eyre* in the *Athenaeum* and and *Spectator* and from the earliest biography of Charlotte Brontë by Mrs. Gaskell down to the blurbs for the reprinting of the novel by the Literary Guild in this country and by Collins in England, we are assured of two points. First, we learn that *Jane Eyre* is probably the great grandmother of all soap operas. It provides strongly affirmative answers to these momentous questions: Can a plain Jane know romance? Can she effectively compete for a man's affections against a dashing, imperious beauty? Can a poor, inexperienced little girl charm a mature man of the world? Can a Cinderella story reoccur in these dull and prosy decades? Second, we are told that *Jane Eyre* is a violently subjective confessional in which a woman proclaims passion equal to that of any man, a passion of even psychic intensity. So perfervid [fervent] an avowal is especially remarkable in a Victorian novelist almost at the midpoint (1847) of the century.

These familiar contentions are quite true, but they do not tell the whole truth about the novel; they do not consider the

Reprinted from Martin S. Day, "Central Concepts in *Jane Eyre*," *The Personalist,* October 1960, with permission.

essential symmetry in the theme of *Jane Eyre.* Like almost all very feminine novelists from Jane Austen to Faith Baldwin (no ranking is intended here), Charlotte Brontë is chiefly concerned with problems of love and marriage. More important in *Jane Eyre* than the soap opera queries above are the questions: What sort of husband should be chosen by a girl of passionate nature and pious lower-middle-class upbringing? For a strong-minded woman what is the proper partnership relation with a husband?

The novel considers the first of these larger questions by confronting the heroine with two males who epitomize in Edward Rochester the marriage partner compatible only through love and in St. John Rivers the marriage partner compatible in all but love. Jane's year of absence from Thornfield is not simply to reverse the fortunes of Jane and Rochester; it is to proffer the heroine the very opposite of potential husband from Rochester. The whole scheme of the novel is missed if the rôle of St. John Rivers is deemed a mere delaying action. Jane must choose between the man who is wrong in all save love, and the man who is right in all save love.

THE POWER OF LOVE

Rochester is the Romantic hero who, as we first meet him, is largely patterned after the meteoric Byron, but also adapted from *Marmion,* which Jane reads in a gift volume incongruously given to her by Rivers. Rochester is a homely libertine, cutting an amorous swath across Europe à la Byron, while a mysterious canker eats at his heart. After the success of the novel, many young Victorian gentlemen copied the manner of Rochester, discovering that even the most staid and prim of young ladies can be attracted to the brusk, ultra-masculine suitor with a spice of wildness in him. Up to the thwarted marriage ceremony, Rochester is incompatible with Jane in age, rank, wealth, and morals—in virtually everything except love. He seems as wrong for her as the prince would be for Cinderella. But when Jane returns to Rochester the tables have been turned with a vengeance. Rochester is now poor, blind, and maimed. He now seems as wrong for her as is a blind beggar would be for a princess. He therefore represents the extremes of incompatibility: he is far above Jane's consideration at the outset, and he is far below her consideration at the end. At either extreme he is bound to Jane solely by the power of love.

St. John Rivers is the Christian hero, drawn after the Rev. Henry Nussey, brother of Ellen Nussey, a friend of Charlotte Brontë. Nussey actually proposed to Charlotte and was rejected, probably for the same reasons that saw the fictional Rivers rejected. Today's readers find Rivers distressingly wooden and unsympathetic. For the Victorian audience Charlotte Brontë apparently felt compelled to delineate him as she did. To the proper Victorian mama with a nubile daughter St. John Rivers would appear to be virtually the ideal husband. He was a Greek God in appearance; he was impeccable in manners and morals; he was strongly intellectual; he was decently provided with this world's goods (largely through Jane's generosity) and super-abundantly provided (we are assured) with otherworldly blessings. Among most middle-class Victorians, where only men were permitted, and certainly not encouraged, to express passion, the ideal man would propose marriage upon a nonpassionate, spiritual plane. It is upon this plane precisely that St. John Rivers offers matrimony to Jane. They are to unite in self-sacrificial Christian service without the low taint of passion. If convinced of Rivers' honesty, a pious Victorian mother would probably urge such a suitor upon a devout daughter. Charlotte works assiduously to affirm the nobility of Rivers and the power of his mind and spirit. Then she must make him so starched, so sermonizing, so humorless, so terribly repressing the natural emotions, that even a Victorian mater is willing to see him dismissed spouseless.

The very conclusion of the novel, the last three paragraphs of the last chapter, are devoted to Rivers; and he is there canonized with the saints and the apostles. Jane seems obviously to be apologizing. Here, she explains, is the noblest of men; but, regrettably, I could not accept his terms. I could not accept union with the handsome, pious Rivers, compatible as he was in all but love. Instead, I prefer Rochester, incompatible in all but the vital essence of love.

JANE'S DILEMMA

With shrewd feminine penetration, the little schoolmarm further realizes that it would be extremely difficult—nay, impossible—to mold St. John Rivers to domesticity.

> As I looked at his lofty forehead, still and pale as a white stone—at his fine lineaments fixed in study—I comprehended all at once that he would hardly make a good hus-

band: that it would be a trying thing to be his wife. I understood, as by inspiration, the nature of his love for Miss Oliver; I agreed with him that it was but a love of the senses. I comprehended how he should despise himself for the feverish influence it exercised over him; how he should wish to stifle and destroy it; how he should mistrust its ever conducing to his happiness, or hers. I saw he was of the material from which nature hews her heroes—Christian and Pagan—her lawgivers, her statesmen, her conquerors: a steadfast bulwark for great interests to rest upon; but, at the fireside, too often a cold, cumbrous column, gloomy and out of place.

The Rochester she has known up to this time, while a magnificent lover, must indeed appear even more intractable as husband material. Strangely enough, the righteous and exemplary Rivers would prove less satisfactory as a spouse than would the dissolute Rochester. Rivers, presumably, represents to Jane a fascinating and repulsive tower of masculine strength that rises above earthly love. Rochester is more humanly weak, vanquished already by the power of love, and at the end yielding to the pattern of domestication.

Although created as opposites almost point by point, the two suitors of Jane have one significant quality in common. The Rochester from whom Jane flees and the Rivers she refuses are both domineering males. Both strive to overpower her will and to rule her. As Rivers is trying to compel her to accept his marriage proposal and accompany him to India, she asserts:

> I was tempted to cease struggling with him—to rush down the torrent of his will into the gulf of his existence, and there lose my own. I was almost as hard beset by him now as I had been once before, in a different way, by another (Rochester). I was a fool both times. To have yielded then would have been an error of principle; to have yielded now would have been an error of judgment.

In the battle of the sexes, Jane, though self-confessedly little, plain, and undistinguished in talents, will not accept the position of inferior.

We now approach the second major element of the novel's theme. Jane Eyre dismisses the loveless but otherwise compatible Rivers for the loving but otherwise incompatible Rochester. What now is to be her marital relationship with her choice?

MARRIAGE THWARTED

Perhaps the most melodramatic chapter in any romance of love is the twenty-sixth chapter of *Jane Eyre*. The tempestuous Rochester and the passionate governess are about to join in wedlock at the altar. As the clergyman asks if there is "any impediment why ye may not lawfully be joined together in matrimony," an objection is startlingly raised by an on-looker. The whole company then sweeps up to the mysteri-ous third floor of Thornfield to find the bestial madwoman, the living wife of Rochester. Deep waters of frustration and despair overwhelm Jane, and the intended wedding, now re-vealed as bigamous, is dramatically snapped off.

Victorian readers could readily conclude that the mad-woman was the symbol of Rochester's ill-spent youth. For his sins he had this horrible weight imposed upon him, and

---

JANE EYRE: A FICTIONAL AUTOBIOGRAPHY

Over the decades, critics have noted that Jane Eyre *re-creates many events of Charlotte Brontë's life. Annette Tromly, who has written extensively on Brontë's fiction, main-tains, however, that the reader should resist the temptation to read the novel as purely autobiographical.*

Evidence that Jane Eyre must not be confused with Charlotte Brontë comes from many sources, among them Brontë's close associates. Harriet Martineau explained in her obituary of Brontë that "Jane Eyre was naturally and universally sup-posed to be Charlotte herself; but she always denied it, calmly, cheerfully, and with the obvious sincerity which characterized all she said." And George Smith, in his *Mem-oirs*, described the painful consequences suffered by Thack-eray after he had, with great insensitivity, introduced Brontë to his mother as "Jane Eyre."

But more intrinsic evidence for the distance between Brontë and her narrator is available. In the act of writing her novel, Brontë was especially careful to separate herself from Jane. The title page of the first edition cited Currer Bell [Brontë's pseudonym] as the editor, not author, of the tale told by Jane Eyre. Brontë herself, then, was even more re-moved from this story than from her first one. Jane Eyre nar-rated, Bell edited, and Brontë remained by choice in the dis-tant background—the invisible begetter of the novel. Given the great amount of care Brontë took to back away from her storyteller, critics should beware of the tendency to take Jane's judgments as direct reflections of the author's.

Annette Tromly, *The Cover of the Mask: The Autobiographers in Charlotte Brontë's Fiction*, 1982.

it remained as the visible bar to his union with Jane. Only when he had suffered for his sins by maiming and disfigurement, only when his sins had been burnt away and his nature had achieved a transforming wholesomeness, only then could he be united with his true love.

Such an interpretation is attractive and, to the usual Victorian, logical. Close examination of the text, however, does not substantiate this hypothesis. Before the lurid revelations of Chapter XXVI there are ample objections to the marriage of Jane and Rochester; however, the basis of these objections is not his sin but the lovers' mutual incompatibility.

The passages between the lovers' wooing and the thwarted marriage contain three types of opposition to the marriage of Jane and Rochester. The first objection comes from Mother Nature, who applauds and condemns in this novel in appropriately Wordsworthian fashion: The horse-chestnut tree beneath which the lovers lyrically romanced is sundered by a thunderbolt into two charred fragments. The second objection springs from persons other than the lovers. The madwoman invades the bedroom of Jane and rends the bridal veil. Mrs. Fairfax appears quite dubious about the marriage. The third objection lies in the doubts and worries of Jane herself. The actions of nature and the presence of the madwoman seem clearly to be symbolic, the stuff of romantic poetry, but the doubts of Mrs. Fairfax and of Jane herself belong to realistic fiction.

In Chapter XXIV the middle-aged housekeeper, Mrs. Fairfax, hears from Jane of her engagement to Rochester. In the midst of a wildly romantic world, the old woman speaks with the voice of prosaic reason and experience:

> How it will answer, I cannot tell; I really don't know. Equality of position and fortune is often advisable in such cases, and there are twenty years of difference in your ages. He might almost be your father.

Here is the crux of the matter. An experienced man of the world, almost forty years of age, wealthy and proud, is to marry a teen-age governess who boasts neither beauty, family, nor wealth. It is a grossly unequal partnership. The whole idea of the marriage originated in the soul of a drab little girl who, from infancy, had been starving for love and affection. The incredible, the impossible, has happened. Pamela is engaged to Mr. B—, the script girl to Clark Gable, Jane to Rochester. But Shakespeare's heroines, we know, often tend to become more realistic as the wedding nears, while his heroes become glassy eyed. In similar manner Jane Eyre now begins to question most searchingly the approaching marriage.

The commonsense doubts of Mrs. Fairfax assail Jane throughout her engagement, and particularly in Chapter XXIV. She doubts that Rochester's ardor will long continue. She imagines that he will weary of her as he has of all previous women in his life. She feels certain that he will weary of showering gifts and favors upon her. She is concerned about their respective stations in life and, most understandably, about their difference in fortune.

> "It would, indeed, be a relief," I thought, "if I had ever so small an independency; I never can bear being dressed like a doll by Mr. Rochester, or sitting like a second Danaë with the golden shower falling daily round me. I will write to Madeira the moment I get home, and tell my uncle John I am going to be married, and to whom: if I had but a prospect of one day bringing Mr. Rochester an accession of fortune, I could better endure to be kept by him now."

The whole passage sounds like a justifiably perturbed fiancée contemplating the sordid facts of married life most realistically.

And how does Rochester behave as the nuptials approach? After he showered gifts upon his fiancée, she states, "His smile was such as a sultan might, in a blissful and fond moment, bestow on a slave his gold and gems had enriched." A few lines later she refuses to dine with him until she is his wife, and Rochester asserts:

> But listen—whisper—it is your time now, little tyrant, but it will be mine presently: and when once I have fairly seized you, to have and to hold, I'll just—figuratively speaking—attach you to a chain like this" (touching his watch-guard). "Yes, bonny wee thing, I'll wear you in my bosom, lest my jewel I should tyne."

The bridegroom-to-be is pictured by the bride-to-be as overbearing and arrogantly superior.

ROCHESTER: A PATERNAL FIGURE

Herein lies the genuine cause for the break-up between Jane and Rochester. She came to his mansion as an 18-year-old governess with little knowledge of life and none of men. In Rochester, twice her age and many times her experience, she had sought a father to love and to be loved by in return.

In one of his earliest protracted conversations with Jane, Rochester points out, "I am old enough to be your father" and his manner thereafter is rather patronizingly paternalistic. In referring to Jane he maintains a steady tattoo of "Little girl," "Little friend," "Child," "Elf," "Little darling," "Childish and slender creature." In Chapter XXIII Rochester glories in his role as protector: "Have I not found her friendless, and cold, and comfortless? Will I not guard, and cherish, and solace her?" Lacking a real father, Jane at first was drawn to the brawny, confident figure of Rochester. He could offer what she had never before known: masculine wisdom of the world, masculine assurance, and masculine protection—in short, the father's role. If marriage should occur as originally planned, he would be the entirely dominant member, the pillar of wealth, strength, and ability, while Jane would be the protected and the ruled, the inferior member of the marriage in every respect; in short, she would be in a daughter's role.

This father-daughter relationship between Rochester and Jane is not satisfactory to her. As Rochester lengthily analyzes her in Chapter XXVIII, under the exterior fragility of Jane stands a monumental strength. "Never," said he, as he ground his teeth, "never was I anything so frail and so indomitable." A woman of weaker spirit would gladly have accepted the role of child to Rochester the father. Jane will not.

Probably every intelligent woman walking the long aisle to where the bridegroom waits will wonder about the marriage she proceeds. Will it work out properly? Is theirs a reasonable and durable partnership? Those women who are not too sure of the answers may here query themselves: Will anyone object at the last moment? Should anyone object? For a girl with Jane's problem the question will almost certainly change to a prayer: "Please, oh please, won't someone object? It's wrong, I tell you. Please object!" In *Jane Eyre*, in the very midst of the wedding ritual, the objector astoundingly leaps forward and Jane is spared a union that she inwardly detests.

THE ROLE OF BERTHA

The chief reason, then, for the existence of the madwoman is to prevent Jane from entering into the wrong partnership with Rochester. Charlotte Brontë had to produce some excuse palatable to herself, to her class, and to her age; so Jane's flight from Rochester appears thoroughly justified when a living wife of Rochester is produced. At the same time the subhuman Bertha Mason makes us sympathize with the bedeviled Rochester.

Those who wish a more psychoanalytical approach (and the intense subjectivity of the novel makes it fair game) may suggest that the madwoman is a projection of Jane. Any sensible observer would be thunderstruck to see Rochester turned down by Jane on the eve of the wedding. An insignificant governess refusing the hand of Mr. Rochester, especially when she says she loves him! The girl must be mad! And the break-up is precisely because of madness, the madwoman embodying the apparent irrationality that permits Jane to escape from Rochester.

When Rochester must reveal all in Chapter XXVII, he asks Jane to elope with him. She pleads conscience to explain her refusal and that excuse would suffice for most 19th century readers, although the novel's theme is the jettisoning of everything else in favor of love. But Jane has other reasons. Realizing how Rochester felt towards his string of mistresses, Jane was convinced that should she "become the successor of these poor girls, he would one day regard me with the same feeling which now in his mind desecrated their memory." Jane will not tolerate a liaison that renders her inferior. She probably feels that even if she were legally wed to rich and powerful Rochester while still the poor, feeble, little Jane Eyre, she would eventually stand in no better position in his eyes than his bought mistresses. She flees from him.

ROLE REVERSAL

She is called back to Rochester when she experiences religious ecstasy combined with passion. In the midst of this trance she telepathically hears her lover calling for her. We later learn that Rochester's cry to her across the many miles occurred when he was undergoing a like experience. Jane is impelled to return because she at last believes that he needs her more than she might need him. Their fortunes have been violently reversed, and she finds Rochester blind and maimed, his left hand amputated. Thornfield and the madwoman have been destroyed. Rochester is poor and friendless, a helpless inmate of unhealthy Ferndean. She now comes to him as an heiress, strong in her youth. Jane is the pillar of wealth, strength, and ability, while Rochester is the protected and the ruled, the inferior member of the marriage, which, in fact, she actually proposed. In Chapter XXXVIII she clearly informs him, "I love you better now, when I can really be useful to you, than I did in your state of proud independence, when you disdained every part but that of the giver and protector."

The roles have now been exactly switched. No longer is Rochester the parent and Jane the child. Now she is the parent and he is the child. In the last chapter of the novel Jane joyfully records:

> Mr. Rochester continued blind the first two years of our union: perhaps it was that circumstance that drew us so very near—that knit us so very close! for I was then his vision, as I am still his right hand. Literally, I was (what he often called me) the apple of his eye. He saw nature—he saw books through me; and never did I weary of gazing for his behalf, and of putting into words the effect of field, tree, town, river, cloud, sunbeam—of the landscape before us; of the wealth round us—and impressing by sound on his ear what light could no longer stamp on his eye. Never did I weary of reading to him; never did I weary of conducting him where he wished to go: of doing for him what he wished to be done. And there was a pleasure in my services, most full, most exquisite, even though sad—because he claimed these services without painful shame or damping humiliation. He loved me so truly, that he knew no reluctance in profiting by my attendance: he felt that I loved him so fondly, that to yield that attendance was to indulge my sweetest wishes.

It is a mother who speaks, a mother lovingly ministering to her child.

Again the psychoanalysts can make much of the maiming of Rochester, which suggests symbolic emasculation, as it most certainly reduces the dominant male to the dependent child. *Jane Eyre* announces the triumph of Love over every obstacle. All else is secondary to the pre-eminence of Love. But the victor is a maternalistic Love that dominates the marriage partnership with its warmth and power.

CHAPTER 4

A Critical Selection

READINGS ON
JANE EYRE

Jane Eyre: A Review

Elizabeth Rigby

The publication of *Jane Eyre* in 1847 met with
sharply divided critical reaction: Elizabeth Rigby's
review was among the most virulent of the negative
analyses. Like many of her Victorian contemporaries, Rigby condemned the controversial novel as
vulgar and immoral. Calling Jane the "personification of an unregenerate and undisciplined spirit,"
Rigby observed that "no Christian grace is perceptible upon her." Interestingly, Rigby cites "incontrovertible" evidence that the novel, which Brontë
wrote under the androgynous pseudonym Currer
Bell, was written by a man.

Jane Eyre is throughout the personification of an unregenerate and undisciplined spirit, the more dangerous to exhibit
from that prestige of principle and self-control which is liable to dazzle the eye too much for it to observe the ineffi-
cient and unsound foundation on which it rests. It is true
Jane does right, and exerts great moral strength, but it is the
strength of a mere heathen mind which is a law unto itself.
No Christian grace is perceptible upon her. She has inherited in fullest measure the worst sin of our fallen nature—
the sin of pride. Jane Eyre is proud, and therefore she is un-
grateful too. It pleased God to make her an orphan,
friendless, and penniless—yet she thanks nobody, and least
of all Him, for the food and raiment, the friends, companions, and instructors of her helpless youth—for the care and
education vouchsafed to her till she was capable in mind as
fitted in years to provide for herself. On the contrary, she
looks upon all that has been done for her not only as her un-
doubted right, but as falling far short of it. The doctrine of
humility is not more foreign to her mind than it is repudi-
ated by her heart. It is by her own talents, virtues, and
courage that she is made to attain the summit of human

Reprinted from Elizabeth Rigby, "Review of *Jane Eyre: An Autobiography,*" *Quarterly
Review,* December 1848.

happiness, and, as far as Jane Eyre's own statement is concerned, no one would think that she owed anything either to God above or to man below. She flees from Mr. Rochester, and has not a being to turn to. Why was this? The excellence of the present institution at Casterton, which succeeded that of Cowan Bridge near Kirkby Lonsdale—these being distinctly, as we hear, the original and the reformed Lowoods of the book—is pretty generally known. Jane had lived there for eight years with 110 girls and fifteen teachers. Why had she formed no friendships among them? Other orphans have left the same and similar institutions, furnished with friends for life, and puzzled with homes to choose from. How comes it that Jane had acquired neither? Among that number of associates there were surely some exceptions to what she so presumptuously stigmatises as "the society of inferior minds." Of course it suited the author's end to represent the heroine as utterly destitute of the common means of assistance, in order to exhibit both her trials and her powers of self-support––the whole book rests on this assumption—but it is one which, under the circumstances, is very unnatural and very unjust.

Altogether the auto-biography of Jane Eyre is pre-eminently an anti-Christian composition. There is throughout it a murmuring against the comforts of the rich and against the privations of the poor, which, as far as each individual is concerned, is a murmuring against God's appointment—there is a proud and perpetual assertion of the rights of man, for which we find no authority either in God's word or in God's providence—there is that pervading tone of ungodly discontent which is at once the most prominent and the most subtle evil which the law and the pulpit, which all civilized society in fact has at the present day to contend with. We do not hesitate to say that the tone of mind and thought which has overthrown authority and violated every code human and divine abroad, and fostered Chartism and rebellion at home, is the same which has also written *Jane Eyre.*

JANE: A VULGAR WOMAN

Still we say . . . this is a very remarkable book. We are painfully alive to the moral, religious, and literary deficiencies of the picture, . . . but it is impossible not to be spellbound with the freedom of the touch. It would be mere hack-

JANE EYRE: A CLEVER NOVEL

Not all early reviewers condemned Jane Eyre. *The following laudatory review of* Jane Eyre *appeared in the* Examiner *in 1847. Although unsigned, many attribute the review to the radical journalist Albany William Fonblanque, who edited and contributed reviews to the* Examiner.

There can be no question but that *Jane Eyre* is a very clever book. Indeed it is a book of decided power. The thoughts are true, sound, and original; and the style, though rude and uncultivated here and there, is resolute, straightforward, and to the purpose. There are faults, which we may advert to presently; but there are also many beauties, and the object and moral of the work is excellent. Without being professedly didactic, the writer's intention (amongst other things) seems to be, to show how intellect and unswerving integrity may win their way, although oppressed by that predominating influence in society which is a mere consequence of the accidents of birth or fortune. There are, it is true, in this autobiography (which though relating to a woman, we do not believe to have been written by a woman), struggles, and throes, and misgivings, such as must necessarily occur in a contest where the advantages are all on one side; but in the end, the honesty, kindness of heart, and perseverance of the heroine, are seen triumphant over every obstacle. We confess that we like an author who throws himself into the front of the battle, as the champion of the weaker party; and when this is followed up by bold and skilful soldiership, we are compelled to yield him our respect.

Whatever faults may be urged against the book, no one can assert that it is weak or vapid. It is anything but a fashionable novel. It has not a Lord Fanny for its hero, nor a Duchess for its pattern of nobility. The scene of action is never in Belgrave or Grosvenor Square. The pages are scant of French and void of Latin. We hear nothing of Madame Maradan; we scent nothing of the bouquet de la Reine. On the contrary, the heroine is cast amongst the thorns and brambles of life;—an orphan; without money, without beauty, without friends; thrust into a starving charity school; and fighting her way as governess, with few accomplishments. The hero, if so he may be called, is (or becomes) middle-aged, mutilated, blind, stern, and wilful. The sentences are of simple English; and the only fragrance that we encounter is that of the common garden flower, or the odour of Mr. Rochester's cigar.

Examiner, November 27, 1847.

neyed courtesy to call it "fine writing." It bears no impress of being written at all, but is poured out rather in the heat and hurry of an instinct, which flows ungovernably on to its object, indifferent by what means it reaches it, and unconscious too. As regards the author's chief object, however, it is a failure—that, namely, of making a plain, odd woman, destitute of all the conventional features of feminine attraction, interesting in our sight. We deny that he has succeeded in this. Jane Eyre, in spite of some grand things about her, is a being totally uncongenial to our feelings from beginning to end. We acknowledge her firmness—we respect her determination—we feel for her struggles; but, for all that, and setting aside higher considerations, the impression she leaves on our mind is that of a vulgar-minded woman—one whom we should not care for as an acquaintance, whom we should not seek as a friend, whom we should not desire for a relation, and whom we should scrupulously avoid for a governess.

There seem to have arisen in the novel-reading world some doubts to who really wrote this book; and various rumours, more or less romantic, have been current in Mayfair, the metropolis of gossip, as to the authorship. For example, *Jane Eyre* is sentimentally assumed to have proceeded from the pen of Mr. Thackeray's governess, whom he had himself chosen as his model of Becky, and who, in mingled love and revenge, personified him in return as Mr. Rochester. In this case, it is evident that the author of *Vanity Fair*, whose own pencil makes him grey-haired, has had the best of it, though his children may have had the worst, having, at all events, succeeded in hitting that vulnerable point in the Becky bosom, which it is our firm belief no man born of woman, from her Soho to her Ostend days, had ever so much as grazed. To this ingenious rumour the coincidence of the second edition of *Jane Eyre* being dedicated to Mr. Thackeray has probably given rise. For our parts, we see no great interest in the question at all. The first edition of *Jane Eyre* purports to be edited by Currer Bell, one of a trio of brothers, or sisters, or cousins, by names Currer, Acton, and Ellis Bell, already known as the joint-authors of a volume of poems. The second edition the same—dedicated, however, "by the author," to Mr. Thackeray; and the dedication (itself an indubitable *chip* of *Jane Eyre*) signed Currer Bell. Author and editor therefore are one, and we are as much satisfied to accept this double individual under the name of "Currer Bell," as under any other, more or less euphonious. Whoever it be, it is a person who, with great mental powers, combines a total ignorance of the habits of society, great coarseness of taste, and a heathenish doctrine of religion. And as these characteristics appear more or less in the writings of all three, Currer, Acton, and Ellis alike, for their poems differ less in degree of power than in kind, we are ready to accept the fact of their identity or of their relationship with equal satisfaction. At all events there can be no interest attached to the writer of *Wuthering Heights*—a novel succeeding *Jane Eyre*, and purporting to be written by Ellis Bell— unless it were for the sake of more individual reprobation. For though there is a decided family likeness between the two, yet the aspect of the Jane and Rochester animals in their native state, as Catherine and Heathfield [sic], is too odiously and abominably pagan to be palatable even to the most vitiated class of English readers. With all the unscrupulousness of the French school of novels it combines that repulsive vulgarity in the choice of its vice which supplies its own antidote. The question of authorship, therefore, can deserve a moment's curiosity only as far as *Jane Eyre* is concerned, and though we cannot pronounce that it appertains to a real Mr. Currer Bell and to no other, yet that it appertains to a man, and not, as many assert, to a woman, we are strongly inclined to affirm. Without entering into the question whether the power of the writing be above her, or the vulgarity below her, there are, we believe, minutiae of circumstantial evidence which at once acquit the feminine hand. No woman—a lady friend, whom we are always happy to consult, assures us—makes mistakes in her own *métier*—no woman *trusses game* and garnishes dessert-dishes with the same hands, or talks of so doing in the same breath. Above all, no woman attires another in such fancy dresses as Jane's ladies assume—Miss Ingram coming down, irresistible, "in a *morning* robe of sky-blue crape, a gauze azure scarf twisted in her hair!!" No lady, we understand, when suddenly roused in the night, would think of hurrying on "*a frock*." They have garments more convenient for such occasions, and more becoming too. This evidence seems incontrovertible. Even granting that these incongruities were purposely assumed, for the sake of disguising the female pen, there is nothing gained; for if we ascribe the book to a woman at all, we have no alternative but to ascribe it to one who has, for some sufficient reason, long forfeited the society of her own sex.

And if by no woman, it is certainly also by no artist. The Thackeray eye has had no part there. There is not more disparity between the art of drawing Jane assumes and her evident total ignorance of its first principles, than between the report she gives of her own character and the conclusions we form for ourselves. Not but what, in another sense, the author may be classed as an artist of very high grade. Let him describe the simplest things in nature—a rainy landscape, a cloudy sky, or a bare moorside, and he shows the hand of a master; but the moment he talks of the art itself, it is obvious that he is a complete ignoramus.

The Cinderella Myth

Charles Burkhart

As other critics have noted, *Jane Eyre* is highly suggestive of a rags-to-riches fairy tale. In the following
selection, Charles Burkhart identifies Brontë's numerous references to the Cinderella myth, a tale im-
proved in Brontë's retelling. At Gateshead, for example, the penniless, orphaned Jane suffers extreme
adversity when she is taken into the home of the
Reeds, the evil stepfamily personified. Just as Cinderella finds Prince Charming, Jane, too, achieves
passionate and everlasting love in her union with
Rochester. In addition to his full-length study of
Brontë's novels, Charles Burkhart has published a
study of English novelist Ivy Compton-Burnett.

The energy of *Jane Eyre* is adolescent, fresh and hopeful; this
thirty-year-old woman's book is "exuberant with the un-
pruned fancies of a girl's mind." For we do not of course lose
what was acquired in one stage of development upon entering another, the second is added to the first: we are infants
in old age, and once adolescent, we are ever after. Jane
speaks of her habitual pre-Rochester reveries as of a tale her
"imagination created, and narrated continuously; quickened
with all of incident, life, fire, feeling, that I desired and had
not in my actual existence" (Chapter 12); it is Charlotte describing the tale of which Jane is heroine; and two or three
pages later Rochester appears, as if to obey the imperatives
of her imagination. Does not daydream continue to dominate our lives? and is not what we call adulthood a stage
only a little more secure in filtering our fantasies with reality? The splendid appeal of the novel is that Jane makes no
concession of any kind to reality. She may say to Rochester
modestly, "Human beings never enjoy complete happiness
in this world. I was not born for a different destiny to the rest
of my species: to imagine such a lot befalling me, is a fairy

Excerpted from *Charlotte Brontë: A Psychosexual Study of Her Novels*, by Charles
Burkhart (London: Victor Gollancz, 1973). Copyright © 1973 by Charles Burkhart.
Reprinted by permission of the publisher.

tale—a day-dream"; but every word is false: her happiness is utter, and her destiny is unique.

Cinderella was a kitchen drudge; Charlotte wrote in a letter, speaking of her own and her heroine's occupation, "I *hate* and *abhor* the very thoughts of governessship". Charlotte took special care in transforming the more unpleasant aspects of her own life. But she transformed all aspects. The fact that she had two sisters and a brother living at the time she was writing her tale may have been so daily a fact as to suggest the dominant pattern of family relationships in the novel. At first they become the wicked step-siblings, Eliza and Georgiana and John; later they are apotheosised into their opposites, Diana and Mary and St. John: the bad Reed cousins become the good Rivers cousins. Another bad lot are the Ingrams—again, like the Reeds, mother, two daughters, son. We do not meet the two Brocklehurst sons, but we briefly encounter the proprietor of Lowood's wife and two daughters.

IMPROVING THE MYTH

The orphan Jane receives a family; the penniless governess becomes an heiress. Her improvements on the myth are shown in just such details: this Cinderella keeps only a quarter of the wealth her uncle leaves her, and divides the rest among her good cousins. Cinderella was presumably pretty once the ashes were wiped away, but Jane is audaciously plain—one of the first plain heroines in the history of the novel: none the less, and here is where Charlotte refines the old legend, Jane becomes pretty, at least in the eyes of the beholder, when she is loved, and Rochester says that, with her shining brown hair and hazel eyes, she is to him a beauty. Jane has it both ways—she is original enough to choose an unhandsome man, no powdered prince in white tights, yet this male plain Jane has a dark virility of broad chest and lean flanks much more attractive than the charming conventional figure. Rochester is wickedly appealing without being wicked; he has the allure of his Restoration namesake, but his philandering with one mistress per country—Céline, Giacinta, and Clara—is a forgivable attempt to forget "that fierce ragout" whom Grace Poole guards under the leads at Thornfield. The nursery tale does not specify if Cinderella after her elevation ever left the palace to patronise her wicked stepsisters with a visit; Jane punishes hers by denying them her own sexual completion: Eliza becomes a

Roman Catholic, which is bad, lives in France, which is worse, and is mother superior of a convent there, worst of all. Georgiana is no nun, but Jane disposes of her in and by marriage to a "wealthy worn-out man of fashion", the key adjective being the second. We are told in the last chapter that Jane has a son; we might have guessed she would bring forth men-children only.

SEXUAL LOVE

The one thing we know specifically about Prince Charming's love for Cinderella was that he admired her feet. Love is what *Jane Eyre* is about; Rochester—disguised as a woman at the moment—says it is "the best of feelings, the highest and the sweetest given to man. . . ." This statement could be found in many a novel. But to define the unique sexual love which Rochester and Jane happily share, there are passages like the following, when Jane is watching Rochester court Blanche:

> I looked, and had an acute pleasure in looking,—a precious, yet poignant pleasure; pure gold, with a steely point of agony: a pleasure like what the thirst-perishing man might feel who knows the well to which he has crept is poisoned, yet stoops and drinks divine draughts nevertheless.

There is a very similar passage in the writings of St. Theresa of Avila; love is, in fact, a religion, in *Jane Eyre.*

One catalyst to the pain/pleasure of love is well understood by Rochester:

> "Well, I feigned courtship of Miss Ingram, because I wished to render you as madly in love with me as I was with you; and I knew jealousy would be the best ally I could call in for the furtherance of that end."

They take turns in tormenting:

> . . . I knew the pleasure of vexing and soothing him by turns; it was one I chiefly delighted in, and a sure instinct always prevented me from going too far: beyond the verge of provocation I never ventured; on the extreme brink I liked well to try my skill.

They seem to exchange male/female roles, as when Rochester says,

> ". . . you please me, and you master me—you seem to submit . . . I am influenced—conquered . . ."

Jane's teasing of Rochester reaches an imaginative height in the month before their (first attempt at) marriage, and he finally threatens her sexually:

" . . . it is your time now, little tyrant, but it will be mine presently . . ."

And Jane has her hesitations before her marriage; Bertha's final descent from the attics, to rip Jane's bridal veil, seems to represent Jane's natural terror at the loss of maidenhead, as her frightening dreams about a young child given into her charge, so well analysed for other meanings by Barbara Hardy in her book on *Jane Eyre*, are striking symbols of her pregnancy fears. Charlotte Brontë's story is in every sense her "secret life".

Supporting the central story are dozens of references to the world of the fairy tale on which it is based. Mystical traditions, superstitions, old wives' legends provide a richly suggestive aura around the Cinderella myth. Rochester's first appearance is preceded by his huge dog Pilot, which to Jane, perched on the stile, resembles the Gytrash, a "North-of-England spirit" figuring in some of Bessie's nursery tales at Gateshead. Rochester seems unable to call Jane a human being: she is elf, changeling, witch, sorceress, fairy—anything but an adult woman. His acceptance of her as real at Ferndean is an acceptance of her equality, even perhaps of her superiority; she does not say, "We were married, reader" but "Reader, I married him".

Jane's Unwholesome Eden

Annette Tromly

Since *Jane Eyre*'s publication, many critics have likened Ferndean—the novel's final setting where Jane achieves a happy union with Rochester—to a lasting Paradise. According to literary critic Annette Tromly, however, any similarities are illusory. Unlike Eden, Tromly asserts, Ferndean is a dismal and stifling setting where happiness is tentative. Furthermore, Jane's proclamations of bliss belie the heroine's inner conflict with the prospect of a complacent, claustrophobic existence at Ferndean. This critical analysis is excerpted from Tromly's book *The Cover of the Mask: The Autobiographers in Charlotte Brontë's Fiction.*

Jane's narrative of a complex lifetime of doubt is resolved by a single moment of epiphany. Although she asserts that Rochester's call makes everything clear for her, the reader has reason to wonder if her certainty was merely "the effect of excitement." If ever a character were ready to be visited by a vision of clarity, it is Jane. Hectored by the missionary zeal of Rivers, she admits that "I was excited more than I had ever been." Significantly, she hears the voice in a dim room which is "full of visions" and "full of moonlight." And if the reader has doubts, it is important to note that Jane, if only momentarily, has doubts of her own. As she hears the voice, she exorcises those doubts by force:

> "Down superstition!" I commented, as that spectre rose up black by the black yew at the gate. "This is not thy deception, nor thy witchcraft: it is the work of nature. She was roused, and did—no miracle—but her best."

With the call in the night, nature and grace finally coalesce for Jane; she feels for the first time that her identity is

Excerpted from chapter 5 of *The Cover of the Mask: The Autobiographers in Charlotte Brontë's Fiction*, by Annette Tromly, English Literary Studies (Victoria, BC: University of Victoria, 1982). Reprinted by permission of the author.

secure: "It was *my* time to assume ascendancy. *My* powers were in play, and in force." Proceeding to Ferndean and to "perfect concord" with Rochester, Jane claims to have found the answer to her uncertainties. For the first time, she feels sure about the path she has taken. Not only has she won the object of her love, but she has also been provided with a meaningful mission: she must spend the rest of her days caring for her blind and crippled husband. As she explains to Rochester, "'I love you better now, when I can really be useful to you, than I did in your state of proud independence, when you disdained every part but that of the giver and protector.'"

CRITICS' RESPONSE

At the end of the novel Jane creates a tableau in which all the conflicting forces within her and within her world are resolved. Most critics have assumed that the resolution is Brontë's as well as Jane's, and have seen it as a convincingly-portrayed moral ideal. Thus Robert Martin writes that "Jane and Rochester, learning to respect the inviolability of the soul as much as earthly delights, become a microcosm of man's striving for Christian reward." And M.H. Scargill sums up the mediative quality of Jane's resolution in his description of her as "neither a profligate nor an ascetic, but a woman who has found an equable solution to the age-old problem. . . ." Indeed, life at Ferndean, for these critics, becomes a "lasting and durable paradise":

> his [Rochester's] and Jane's reunion takes place against a benign background of profuse vegetation, and life-giving water bathes Ferndean when she arrives. The name itself, meaning "fern valley". . . supplies a benediction connoting shelter and repose.

> a happy ending which even the most cynical critic cannot find inappropriate. . . . But this is a fortunate fall because she eventually re-enters . . . a more lasting and durable paradise at Ferndean.

> . . . Miss Brontë never wrote a more sure and successful scene than this reunion of lovers battered by life. . . . Like an echo of the end of *Paradise Lost* they enter a new life, putting behind them the illicit Eden of the garden at Thornfield, all forbidden passion spent.

These critics rightly respond to the rich texture of Miltonic allusion in the novel's final chapters. But the relationship of *Jane Eyre* to *Paradise Lost* is perhaps more complicated than their comments would allow.

A CURIOUS PARADISE

In their rush to liken Ferndean to Milton's Eden, these critics have overlooked the many ironies which Brontë has planted in Jane's paradise. The Rochesters' Eden has as its setting a place so "insalubrious" that even Bertha was not sent there. Ferndean is in an overgrown valley, with no sense of prospect, "no opening anywhere." The house in which Jane and Rochester will live partakes of the confinement of the setting: "the windows were latticed and narrow: the front-door was narrow, too. . . ." Compared to the ending of *Paradise Lost*, where the "world was all before" Adam and Eve, this world is tightly enclosed, even claustrophobic. It is a curious place indeed for a happy ending.

Having struggled through dense foliage to Ferndean, Jane first sees Rochester as she stands in enclosed ground. Ferndean, like Thornfield, is, an illusory fairy-land. Ferndean's creatures, however, differ in one important respect from the fairy and hero of the early novel: Jane and Rochester have completely reversed their roles. The caged bird of earlier days is no longer Jane, but Rochester; the saviour who will attempt to liberate the bird, no longer Rochester, but Jane. For Jane the new roles are a gratifying resolution no longer subject to the humiliations of her "giver and protector," she can assume the role herself: "prop and guide." The solution is not quite as unambiguous as Jane supposes. The reader notes that Rochester, for example, whose sin was that he tried to make his own fate, now merely makes Jane his fate: the difference is hardly substantive. And as Rochester's eyes, Jane will not only interpret his world to him, she will thoroughly determine his point of view. It is with skepticism about both of the lovers' futures that we note this reversal of roles in Jane's latest form of enclosure: ". . . I arrested his wandering hand, and prisoned it in both mine." The bird is not caged, but prisoned; his keeper is his jailer. Neither will be set free.

If the fairy-tale has been turned upside-down, it has also been turned inside-out: the fanciful has become literal. What began as an imaginative construct—Jane's childish image in a mirror, which was filtered through Bessie's stories, enlarged by adolescent daydreams, and secured in portraits—is now completely a matter of the everyday. We wonder, as we contemplate the Rochesters' future, what Jane will *do* with herself at Ferndean, especially when we learn that Rochester is regaining his eyesight; not even noble self-sacrifice will be a lasting possibility for Jane. The chilling thought of day-to-day life at Ferndean brings to mind Adèle's early warning that Jane would tire of living on the moon with Rochester. We can only imagine Jane looking backward, not forward—trying to reconstruct, through her autobiography, a life that has nowhere else to go.

The dismal prospects of everyday life at Ferndean are intensified by the very force of Jane's protestations of unending bliss:

> I know no weariness of my Edward's society: he knows none of mine, any more than we each do of the pulsation of the heart that beats in our separate bosoms; consequently, we are ever together. To be together is for us to be at once as free as in solitude, as gay as in company. We talk, I believe, all day long: to talk to each other is but a more animated and an audible thinking. All my confidence is bestowed on him; all his confidence is devoted to me: we are precisely suited in character; perfect concord is the result.

Jane's hyperbolic description of her happiness betrays the same complacency that she has confronted in other people so often. She speaks glibly on behalf of her husband; her repeated assertions that they are one have the effect of making Rochester disappear. And she also condescends to Rochester: as she "bestows" confidence on him, he "devotes" it to her. Characteristically, Jane attempts in this passage to make mythic what is ordinary—and in the process forces experience into a formula. But by means of her inflationary rhetoric, she inadvertently undercuts her own fictive Eden. The perfect concord she claims to have found is inconceivable outside the gates of Paradise.

Jane's new-found complacency extends to others besides Rochester. The attitudes she expresses at the end of her autobiography about the young Adèle, for example, sound disturbingly like the attitudes Mrs. Reed once held about the young Jane Eyre. Years earlier Mrs. Reed had been unable to summon regard for an "uncongenial alien":

> how could she really like an interloper not of her race, and unconnected with her, after her husband's death, by any tie? It must have been most irksome to find herself bound by a hard-wrung pledge to stand in the stead of a parent to a strange child she could not love, and to see an uncongenial alien permanently intruded on her own family group.

Although she seems to have become the model child that Jane never could be, Adèle is nevertheless being judged by the same cold standards:

> As she grew up, a sound, English education corrected in a great measure her French defects; and when she left school, I found in her a pleasing and obliging companion: docile, good-tempered and well-principled. By her grateful attention to me and mine, she has long since well repaid any little kindness I ever had it in my power to offer her.

Jane's self-satisfied condescension to the child echoes the bloodless attitude of her own first guardian; in becoming Mrs. Rochester, she has somehow dissolved into Mrs. Reed. Adèle's unfortunate situation delicately insinuates itself into Jane's happy ending.

Despite Jane's self-proclaimed sense of fulfillment, the final paragraphs of the novel reveal that her psychic equipoise is tentative. At centre stage when the story closes is not, as we might expect, the perfect concord of the Rochesters, but rather the zealous martyrdom of St. John Rivers. As Hunsden's physical presence disturbed the domestic tranquility of the Crimsworths, so Rivers' spiritual presence threatens Jane's peace. Jane's last words in her autobiography shatter her tone of pastoral contentment; while contemplating the fate of Rivers, she adopts his own frenetic idiom:

> A more resolute, indefatigable pioneer never wrought amidst rocks and dangers. Firm, faithful, and devoted; full of energy, and zeal, and truth, he labours for his race: he clears their painful way to improvement; he hews down like a giant the prejudices of creed and caste that encumber it. He may be stern; he may be exacting; he may be ambitious yet: but his is the sternness of the warrior Greatheart, who guards his pilgrim-convoy from the onslaught of Apollyon. His is the exaction of the apostle, who speaks but for Christ, when he says—"Whosoever will come after me, let him deny himself, and take up his cross and follow me." His is the ambition of the high master-spirit, which aims to fill a place in the first rank of those who are redeemed from the earth—who stand without fault before the throne of God; who share the last mighty victories of the lamb; who are called, and chosen, and faithful.

Jane's imagination is ignited by Rivers' grand commitment and by his absolute certainty of the path he has taken. Something within her compares the epic scale of Rivers' mission with her pedestrian existence at Ferndean and an abyss of uncertainty opens before her—despite her protestations to the contrary. When she notes that in the hour of Rivers' death, "his mind will be unclouded; his heart will be undaunted; his hope will be sure; his faith steadfast," Jane attributes to him the certainty which she has always desired. We realize that life at Ferndean will not provide this certainty. If she has finally gained control of two lives, Jane can hardly master her own emotional equilibrium. Like William Crimsworth, she has transformed her outer life—but her inner life remains as unsettled as it has always been.

The sense of satisfying closure which Jane claims in her autobiography's final chapters, then, is qualified by the reader's sense of her claustrophobia. For rather than beginning her life at Ferndean, she seems to be living her death instead. Nothing remains for her to do with herself. She can only revitalize a static life by writing it; she can only attempt a resurrection by turning to autobiography.

The autobiography she produces, however, seems to be something that was conceived on Thornfield's third story. We recall her earlier remarks:

> my sole relief was to walk along the corridor of the third story, backwards and forwards . . . and allow my mind's eye to dwell on whatever bright visions rose before it . . . and, best of all, to open my inward ear to a tale that was never ended—a tale my imagination created, and narrated continuously. . . .

Walking backwards and forwards along the corridor of her life, Jane has created one of her elevated tales that never ended. She has settled finally for the easy complacency of a myth predicated on happy endings. And as Brontë implies, such happy endings occur only in fiction—in imaginary, prelapsarian [before the fall of man] worlds which are unacquainted with life's unavoidable ambiguity. Through her art, Jane has deluded herself. For the sake of a narrow clarity, she has clung to her "bright visions," forsaken her keen awareness of complexity. If Jane Eyre needs her clarity, however, Charlotte Brontë does not let it stand unqualified. She answers Jane's unworldly fiction with her own severe Truth. At the last moment, as Jane thinks of Rivers from Ferndean, an uninvited visitor seems to intrude into the carefully arranged chamber of her mind: Jane is not in fact free from either doubt or desire. Brontë implies that the last door will remain ajar; Jane cannot lock up her truth in fiction.

Jane Eyre: A Contemporary Heroine

Erica Jong

In the introduction to the Penguin edition of *Jane Eyre*, Erica Jong writes that Charlotte Brontë was ahead of her time in her creation of the unforgettable heroine Jane. Brontë, according to Jong, convincingly—if not consciously—portrays a woman who refuses to succumb to the rules and strictures imposed on nineteenth-century women. Rather, Jane's strivings are remarkably modern: With unswerving courage, Jane breaks the conventions of Victorian society in her quest for independence, self-respect, and a love relationship based on equality. Jong, the author of six best-selling novels, speaks frequently on issues that affect women.

When a book is beloved by readers and hated by contemporary critics, we should suspect that a revolution in consciousness is in progress. This was certainly the case with *Jane Eyre*. The pseudonymous author, Currer Bell, was blamed for committing the "highest moral offence a novel writer can commit, that of making an unworthy character interesting in the eyes of a reader." The book was said to be mischievous and vulgar, pandering to the public's taste for "illegitimate romance." As for the character of the heroine, "Jane Eyre is throughout the personification of an unregenerate and undisciplined spirit . . . she has inherited in fullest measure the worst sin of our fallen nature—the sin of pride."

These criticisms were put forth by a woman reviewer, Elizabeth Rigby, in *The Quarterly Review* in 1848, four years after the novel was published, when it was already a roaring success. The same critic took pains to dispute the rumor that

Currer Bell was a woman, explaining that the descriptions of cookery and fashion could not have come from a female pen. She also argued that the book would do more harm than good to governesses, and for good measure, she condemned Jane Eyre as one "whom we should not care for as an acquaintance, whom we should not seek as a friend, whom we should not desire for a relation, and whom we should scrupulously avoid for a governess."

Such character assassinations would be too absurd to quote if they did not foreshadow the charges against every important novel of the nineteenth and twentieth centuries that depicted a woman as a complex human being rather than a stereotype. More than that, they foreshadow contemporary assaults on women's anger, rebellion, and nonconformity—whether exemplified in fiction or in life. For Jane is nothing if not a rebel. She will not lie even if lies would smooth her progress. From the moment we meet her, she is struggling against the injustice of her lot, and she refuses to be convinced that humility is her only option. In many ways she is the first modern heroine in fiction.

SELF-RESPECT

The perennial popularity of *Jane Eyre* with readers is surely based on Jane's indomitable spirit. Given every reason to feel crushed, discouraged, beaten, Jane's will remains unbroken. Neither beautiful nor rich nor supplied with a cossetting family, Jane seems to be possessed of the greatest treasure a woman can have: self-respect. That alone makes her an inspiring heroine. No one can take away her inner self-esteem. It is apparent from the very start of the book, when ten-year-old Jane tells her supposed "benefactress" Mrs. Reed (who has unjustly punished her by secluding her from her cousins): "They are not fit to associate with me." We love Jane because she seems to know her own worth—an unforgivable thing in girls and women.

It is her grittiness that saves her at Lowood school, where punishments are meted out unfairly and girls are sent to starve and sicken. Helen, who meekly accepts unjust punishments, dies. Jane survives because she does not. In fact, it is remarkable how often Jane says the thing she knows she should not as if overcome by an irresistible force. She is active where all her training tells her to be passive. She speaks the truth when she is supposed to flatter. She longs

VICTORIAN PROPRIETY

As Winifred Gerin explains in her book The Brontës: The Creative Works, *Brontë boldly departed from Victorian convention when she created the independent and passionate heroine Jane.*

Reminded by Rochester that she has no one to be injured or offended by any act of hers, since she is alone in the world—'. . . Who in the world cares for *you*? or who will be injured by what you do?' he pleads. '*I* care for myself', answers Jane. 'The more solitary, the more friendless, the more unsustained I am, the more I will respect myself. . . .'

With that reply Rochester's attempted seduction crumbles; he has no argument to oppose it. He is answered by an equal in judgement and a superior in honour. It was the second time in the book that the author claimed equality for her heroine with her hero. The first occasion was when Jane anticipated Rochester's declaration of love by avowing her own feelings for him. It was so novel a departure from the conventional canons of fiction, that it shocked and startled the literary establishment, and the book's first readers. It was considered a grossly coarse thing for a woman to declare her love for a man—and for an author to describe it—even if he were a reputedly male author like Currer Bell. Jane Eyre committed two faults against Victorian female delicacy when she declared her love—as yet unsolicited—for one man, and rejected another, later in the book, on the score of *not* loving him. Such statements were tantamount to admitting a knowledge of the passion of love not permissible in a decent woman. Hence the savage comment by Elizabeth Rigby who, reviewing *Jane Eyre* in *The Quarterly* (December 1848), expressed the opinion that if the unknown author of *Jane Eyre* were a woman, as some suspected, then she was one who must have forfeited the society of her own sex.

What Currer Bell had done, and what many of her female contemporaries could not forgive her for, was to place truth before propriety, and to recognize the equality of the sexes where passion was concerned. Without being in any way 'a feminist' in the militant sense of the word, Charlotte Brontë felt deeply about the oppressed status of women in her time, especially women endowed with intelligence but devoid of fortune or looks, like herself. She made *their* predicament her own when she chose to write a novel about a governess with a mind infinitely superior to her employers.

Winifred Gerin, *The Brontës: The Creative Works*, 1964.

for the wide world when she is supposed to be content with her narrow lot. "I could not help it; the restlessness was in my nature," she says, pacing "backwards and forwards" on the third story of Thornfield Hall. "Women feel just as men feel," Jane says, "they need exercise for their faculties and a field for their efforts."

When a book has been copied as much as *Jane Eyre*, has spawned as many bad imitations, movies, adaptations, it's necessary to go back to the text and try to see it as if for the first time. What has usually been imitated about this novel is not the spirit of the heroine but the gloomy house with its dark secret, its glowering hero, and the star-crossed romance of its two principal characters. These strike me as the *least* important elements of the story. If Jane were a passive heroine, neither the romantic battlements of gloomy Thornfield nor the curmudgeonly charms of Mr. Rochester would capture us. But Jane's bluntness, the modernity of her strivings for independence, invite us into the tale. From the first instant we meet Jane Eyre, we know she is a different breed.

As a novelist, what interests me most about *Jane Eyre* is the way Charlotte Brontë transformed autobiographical materials to create a myth that is larger and more powerful than any of its parts. Apparently Charlotte and her siblings did have a forbidding aunt who attempted without success to replace their dead mother. Apparently they were sent away to a harsh charity school not unlike Lowood. Apparently, Charlotte did fall in love with a married man—M. Heger, the headmaster of the school in Brussels where Charlotte, for a time, taught. But the way Charlotte *changed* these materials is far more interesting than the way the facts agree with her autobiography. She sets the struggle not in a school in Brussels but in a foreboding North of England country house where the restless master comes and goes. The house represents the fate of woman in the nineteenth century: enclosure, entrapment, no hope of escape. Not only Jane is captive there, but so is Jane's alter ego, Bertha Mason, the mad wife in the attic. And the mystery revolves around the discovery of the mad wife, whose existence is denied even when her rages threaten the lives of those in the house.

ENTRAPPED WOMANHOOD

It was Charlotte Brontë's genius to find a threefold representation of nineteenth-century woman: the feisty Jane, the animalistic Bertha, the mansion that is destined to burn down because of its incendiary contents. If Bertha is sexuality denied, then Jane is freedom denied, but they are both aspects of entrapped womanhood. Thornfield Hall itself represents the outdated rules imposed on women—which cannot endure any more than a house with a trapped madwoman can.

Surely all these symbols were unconscious with the author. Otherwise she could not have made them so convincing. But the unconscious of an artist is her greatest treasure. It is what transmutes the dross of autobiography into the gold of myth.

Jane Eyre takes the form of a pilgrimage in which a little girl who is old before her time from being reared in the most constricted of circumstances gradually finds a way to blossom. But first she must submit to many tests. She must reject a variety of hypocritical masculine figures who feel it is their right to rule her. She must reject the fate of being a female victim—the only model presented to her by other women. She must reject the entreaties of her potential lover until he has been transformed by his own purifying odyssey.

To be the equal of Jane Eyre, Rochester must renounce all other women, see his patrimony go up in flames, lose an eye and a hand, and become grateful where he once was arrogant. Only when he has been thus transformed can he and Jane have a happily-ever-after.

Charlotte Brontë's brilliance was to create a myth which is the embodiment of female wish fulfillment. The universe of *Jane Eyre* operates according to female laws. Jane's success as a heroine depends on her breaking all the rules decreed for nineteenth-century women. Outspoken where she should be submissive, bold where she should be grateful—apparently nobody has told Jane Eyre that she is plainer than Cinderella's step-sisters and has no business turning down a rich suitor before she knows she is an heiress herself. This is a fairy tale that reverses all the rules of fairy tales. No wonder it strikes readers as a burst of light into the heart of darkness.

DREAMS AND VISIONS

To a remarkable extent, the novel relies on the heroine's sensitivity to dreams and visions—as if the author were saying that only a woman in touch with her deepest dreams can be a strong survivor in a world so toxic to women. Dreams are crucial in *Jane Eyre*. The night before Jane is to marry the already married Rochester, she prophetically dreams that "Thornfield Hall was a dreary ruin, the retreat of bats and owls." The house is reduced to "a shell-like wall, very high and fragile-looking," and Jane wanders there with an unknown child in her arms.

Perhaps the child in the dream represents the innocence that she is soon to lose. At church the next day, the wedding is canceled when Rochester's bigamy is revealed. Because he thinks of Bertha Mason as a "clothed hyena" whom he was entrapped into marrying, Rochester has no qualms about betraying his mad wife. But Jane, though she loves him, refuses to be drawn into his error. He married Bertha for her money, and that falsehood is not so easily cured. In this female universe, a man is not forgiven for a cynical marriage even if it is the rule in his society. So Jane, though heartbroken, leaves Thornfield Hall. She wanders in the dark woods of her destiny, finds she is an heiress herself, is commandeered in marriage by another man (the dour parson, St. John) while Rochester's soul is being shriven.

Rochester may be arrogant and full of male entitlement, but he is not cold and calculating like St. John. In fact, it is St. John who evokes in Jane the certainty that she can only marry for love. He wants Jane because she will make a good missionary in India, not because he loves her. This Jane feels as "an iron shroud contracted round me." She can't allow herself to be with a man whose brow is "commanding but not open," whose eyes are "never soft." By refusing to marry him, "I should still have my unblighted self to turn to: my natural unenslaved feelings with which to communicate in moments of loneliness. There would be recesses in my mind which would be only mine." As his wife she would become "the imprisoned flame" consumed from within.

Jane may be the first heroine in fiction to know that she needs her own identity more than she needs marriage. Her determination not to relinquish selfhood for love could well belong to a contemporary heroine.

Jane can only return to Rochester when she can say: "I am an independent woman now." And she can only surrender to him when he says: "All the melody on earth is concentrated in Jane's tongue to my ear." "The water stood in my eyes to hear the avowal of his dependence," Jane says. And indeed she cannot marry Rochester until he knows he is as dependent on her as she is on him. Their odysseys have equalized them: Jane has become an independent woman and Rochester has been cured of entitlement. Only thus can a woman and man become equals in a patriarchal society.

We are drawn to those myths that speak the truth we know about our inner lives. *Jane Eyre* endures because it tells the truth about what makes a marriage of two minds possible. The shoe fits—far better than Cinderella's glass slipper. Men must be stripped of arrogance and women must become independent for any happily-ever-after to endure between the sexes. Charlotte Brontë's unconscious was way ahead of her time.

Chronology

1816

Charlotte Brontë is born to the Reverend Patrick Brontë and Maria Branwell on April 21 in Thornton, England, the third of six children.

1817

Patrick Branwell Brontë is born in June.

1818

In February, Charlotte's mother, Maria, becomes ill; Emily Brontë is born in July.

1820

Anne Brontë is born in January; family moves to Haworth, Yorkshire, where Reverend Brontë is appointed curate.

1821

Maria Branwell dies of cancer.

1824

Charlotte and her sisters Maria, Elizabeth, and Emily attend the Cowan Bridge Clergy Daughters' School in Lancashire.

1825

Maria and Elizabeth die of tuberculosis; Charlotte and Emily return home.

1826–1831

The Brontë children begin their imaginative play with (Patrick) Branwell's toy soldiers; children chronicle their games and plays in various forms.

1829

Charlotte and Branwell begin writing sagas about an imaginary kingdom they call Angria.

1831–1832

Charlotte attends Roe Head School; meets lifelong friend Ellen Nussey, who preserves hundreds of Charlotte's letters, used extensively by biographers after Charlotte's death.

1832–1835

Charlotte returns home to oversee her sisters' education; continues writing the mythical Angrian sagas with Branwell.

1835–1838

Charlotte returns to Roe Head School as a teacher, a position she does not enjoy.

1836

Charlotte submits poems to Robert Southey, poet laureate; receives discouraging reply.

1838

Coronation of Queen Victoria; publication of *Oliver Twist* by Charles Dickens.

1839

Charlotte rejects marriage proposal of Reverend Henry Nussey in March; accepts a post as governess for the Sidgewick family but leaves within a year; rejects a second suitor, Reverend David Bryce, in August.

1841

Charlotte takes on a new position as a governess for the White family; finds the post unbearable and quits.

1842

Charlotte and Emily travel to Brussels to study at the Pensionnat Heger, where the demanding headmaster, Constantin Heger, recognizes Charlotte's literary talent; the sisters return home when their aunt dies in November.

1843

Charlotte returns alone to Brussels; falls deeply in love with M. Heger; becomes depressed and lonely because M. Heger does not return her love; writes poetry.

1844

Charlotte returns home; attempts and fails to open a school in Haworth.

1845

Branwell begins serious decline into alcoholism and opium addiction; the sisters plan a joint publication of poetry under the pseudonyms Currer, Ellis, and Acton Bell.

1846

Sisters publish, at their own expense, *Poems* by Currer, Ellis, and Acton Bell; sell two copies; Charlotte submits for publication *The Professor,* which chronicles her experiences in Brussels, but is rejected six times; Charlotte begins writing *Jane Eyre;* Emily writes *Wuthering Heights;* Anne writes *Agnes Grey.*

1847

Publication of *Wuthering Heights* by Emily (Ellis Bell); publication of *Agnes Grey* by Anne (Acton Bell); publication of *Jane Eyre* by Charlotte (Currer Bell); *Jane Eyre* is an immediate success, fueling intense public curiosity about the identity of the Bells; Charlotte begins correspondence with prominent critic George Henry Lewes.

1848

Charlotte dedicates second edition of *Jane Eyre* to novelist William Makepeace Thackeray, sparking rumors that the author was the governess employed by Thackeray; literary community speculates that the Bells are the same person; Charlotte and Anne travel to London to prove their separate identities; Anne's *The Tenant of Wildfell Hall* published; Branwell dies of tuberculosis in September; Emily contracts the same illness and dies in December; Anne, too, becomes seriously ill; Thackeray's *Vanity Fair* published.

1849

Anne dies in May; devastated by the deaths of her siblings, Charlotte throws herself into writing *Shirley,* which is published to mixed reviews; travels to London where she meets her literary idol, Thackeray, and the feminist social critic Harriet Martineau.

1850

Charlotte becomes friends with the novelist Elizabeth Gaskell, who will become Charlotte's official biographer; writes prefaces to posthumous editions of *Wuthering Heights* and *Agnes Grey.*

1851

Charlotte rejects marriage proposal of James Taylor; begins writing *Villette.*

1852

Charlotte rejects marriage proposal of Reverend Arthur Nicholls, curate at Haworth.

1853

Villette published to favorable reviews.

1854

Charlotte marries Nicholls in June; the two honeymoon in Ireland; Crimean War begins.

1855

Charlotte, now pregnant, contracts tuberculosis; Charlotte and her unborn child die on March 31.

1857

Publication of Elizabeth Gaskell's sympathetic biography, *The Life of Charlotte Brontë,* establishes the Brontë legend; posthumous publication of *The Professor.*

1861

Patrick Brontë dies.

1906

Arthur Nicholls dies.

FOR FURTHER RESEARCH

ABOUT CHARLOTTE BRONTË AND *JANE EYRE*

Miriam Allott, ed., *The Brontës: The Critical Heritage*. London: Routledge & Kegan Paul, 1974.

Juliet Barker, *The Brontës*. London: Weidenfeld and Nicolson, 1994.

Patricia Beer, *Reader I Married Him*. London: Macmillan, 1974.

Harold Bloom, ed., *Modern Critical Views: The Brontës*. New York: Chelsea House, 1987.

Charles Burkhart, *Charlotte Brontë: A Psychosexual Study of Her Novels*. London: Victor Gollancz, 1973.

R.W. Crump, *Charlotte and Emily Brontë: A Reference Guide*. Boston: G.K. Hall, 1982.

Richard J. Dunn, ed., *Charlotte Brontë: Jane Eyre*. New York: Norton, 1971.

Enid Duthie, *The Foreign Vision of Charlotte Brontë*. London: Macmillan, 1975.

Barbara and Gareth Lloyd Evans, *The Scribner Companion to the Brontës*. New York: Scribner, 1982.

Juliet Gardiner, ed., *The Brontës at Haworth: The World Within*. New York: Crown, 1993.

Elizabeth Gaskell, *The Life of Charlotte Brontë*. New York: Penguin Classics, 1975.

Winifred Gerin, *Charlotte Brontë: The Evolution of Genius*. Oxford: Clarendon Press, 1967.

Lyndall Gordon, *Charlotte Brontë: A Passionate Life*. New York: W.W. Norton & Co., 1994.

Ian Gregor, *The Brontës: A Collection of Critical Essays*. Englewood Cliffs, NJ: Prentice-Hall, 1970.

Jeanette King, *Jane Eyre*. Philadelphia: Open University Press, 1986.

Cynthia A. Linder, *Romantic Imagery in the Novels of Charlotte Brontë*. New York: Harper & Row, 1978.

John Maynard, *Charlotte Brontë and Sexuality.* Cambridge: Cambridge University Press, 1984.

Judith O'Neill, ed., *Critics on Charlotte and Emily Brontë.* London: George Allen & Unwin, 1968.

Anne Passal, *Charlotte and Emily Brontë: An Annotated Bibliography.* New York: Garland, 1979.

Margot Peters, *Charlotte Brontë: Style in the Novel.* Madison: University of Wisconsin Press, 1973.

_____, *Unquiet Soul: A Biography of Charlotte Brontë.* New York: Doubleday, 1975.

Fannie E. Ratchford, *The Brontës' Web of Childhood.* New York: Columbia University Press, 1941.

Norman Sherry, *Literary Critiques: Charlotte and Emily Brontë.* New York: Arco, 1970.

Clement Shorter, ed., *The Brontës: Life and Letters.* London: Hodder and Stroughton, 1969.

Tom Winnifrith, *The Brontës and Their Background: Romance and Reality.* London: Macmillan, 1973.

Thomas James Wise and John Alexander Symington, eds., *The Brontës: Their Lives, Friendships, and Correspondence.* Oxford: Basil Blackwell, 1980.

H.E. Wroot, *The Persons and Places of the Brontë Novels.* New York: Burt Franklin, 1970.

WORKS BY THE AUTHOR

Jane Eyre: An Autobiography. Edited by Currer Bell. London: Smith, Elder, 1847.

Charlotte Brontë, *Jane Eyre.* With an introduction by Humphrey Ward. London: J. Murray, 1920.

_____, *Jane Eyre.* With an introduction by William Peden. New York: Modern Library, 1950.

_____, *Jane Eyre.* With a critical and biographical profile of Charlotte Brontë by Inga Stina Ewbank. New York: Franklin Watts, 1969.

_____, *Jane Eyre.* With an introduction by Basil Davenport. New York: Dodd Mead & Co., 1979.

_____, *Jane Eyre.* Edited and with background and critical notes by Richard J. Dunn. New York: Norton, 1987.

_____, *Jane Eyre.* With an introduction and notes by Michael Mason. New York: Penguin Books, 1996.

HISTORICAL BACKGROUND FOR VICTORIAN ENGLAND

Nina Auerback, *Woman and the Demon: The Life of a Victorian Myth.* Cambridge, MA: Harvard University Press, 1982.

Amy Cruse, *The Victorians and Their Reading.* Cambridge, MA: Riverside Press, 1963.

Valentine Cunningham, *Everywhere Spoken Against: Dissent in the Victorian Novel.* Oxford: Clarendon Press, 1975.

L. Elliot-Binns, *Religion in the Victorian Era.* London: Lutterworth Press, 1936.

Walter E. Houghton, *The Victorian Frame of Mind.* New Haven, CT: Yale University Press, 1966.

Sally Mitchell, *Daily Life in Victorian England.* Westport, CT: Greenwood Press, 1996.

Joan Perkin, *Victorian Women.* New York: New York University Press, 1995.

Lionel Stevenson, ed., *Victorian Fiction: A Guide to Research.* New York: Modern Language Association, 1964.

Martha Vicinus, *Suffer and Be Still: Women in the Victorian Age.* Bloomington: Indiana University Press, 1973.

INDEX